Good Dog? Bad Dog?

By Rosie Barclay

(BSc(Hons) MPhil CCAB)

Animal Behaviourist

Dedication

A huge thank you to my far from "perfect" Airedale Lowry-dog who has helped hundreds of dogs overcome their fear of other dogs. He happily ignored them all.

Also to my husband Iain for becoming a computer screen widow and to my children Dylan and Chloe for putting up with the countless remarks of "I'm working"!

And finally to all my clients and their dogs for making my work-life a constant challenge and a joy.

Good Dog? Bad Dog?

(A fresh look at how we treat our dogs)

Introduction

Some dogs behave perfectly most of the time, others for some of the time and for a few, none of the time. For some owners the thought of even walking along the road with their dog evokes fears of nightmarish proportions. For others simply leaving their dog home alone for a few hours' results in hundreds of pounds worth of damage. For a few it is the fear and shame of yet another vets bill because their dog has damaged somebody else's better behaved pet. So can we aspire to the dizzy heights of perfection? Or are we expecting too much from our beloved companions? Do we really need or want to own the "perfect" dog and just what is "perfect" behaviour anyway?

For many years the "perfect" dog was one that:
- ➤ Obediently walked close to their owners legs.
- ➤ Did not react to other approaching dogs or people especially children.
- ➤ Did not bark unless someone was trying to break into the house.
- ➤ Saved many an owner from certain death by fire.
- ➤ Chased a ball thrown by its owners, brought it promptly back and all in one piece.
- ➤ Sat when told, laid down, rolled over, came back and played dead for the queen.
- ➤ Was utterly obedient and under its owners "control" at all times or else it was throttled by the neck with a metal choke chain.

A tall order for most dogs and many fell by the wayside ending up in the numerous rescue centres that were springing up around the country. Nowadays, much of our philosophy and our ideals of how dogs are supposed to behave have changed. Instead of treating them as unruly humans we now try to understand them as dogs and look at how they behave naturally with each other. However, my experience as a clinical companion animal behaviourist has led me to realise that the more "traditional" views still remain strongly embedded in our minds and are still taught in some institutions around the country.

More recently there has been another train of thought suggesting that owners should dominate their dogs by behaving as if they were the "Top Dog" in the pack and that this will cure all conceivable problems. This view can be misleading and may sometimes have grave consequences.

> So why are we still getting it wrong?
> Why are so many dogs ending up in rescue centres or being put to sleep?
> Why are dogs and their owners still suffering from what we perceive as imperfect behaviour?

This book concentrates on changing the traditional views of how we perceive and treat our dogs using what we have learned from scientific research so far. By gaining a better understanding of why your dog behaves in certain ways you will begin to view your canine friend in a very different light and hopefully come to realise that none of us are or ever will be perfect.

The book starts at the beginning by looking at ways of how to chose and bring up a new puppy that may reduce the likelihood of future problems. It then goes on to cover different problems that commonly occur between owners and their maturing or adult dogs by discussing real case studies.

These problems include:
- ➢ Aggressive behaviour towards people and other dogs.
- ➢ Destructive behaviour when home alone.
- ➢ Nervousness.
- ➢ Attention seeking behaviour.
- ➢ Loss of toilet control.
- ➢ Aggressive behaviour towards other family dogs.
- ➢ It also covers basic unruly behaviour such as stealing, eating things it shouldn't, chasing other animals and lack of recall.

Each chapter emphasises the complexities of each set of problems, the different approaches used in trying to solve them and the underlying factors that may have caused them to occur in the first place. It is important to remember that each case is individual and that the diagnosis and treatment will not always be the same for a similar problem that another owner may be experiencing. If you are encountering a challenging problem it is wise to consult a fully qualified companion animal behaviourist referred by your veterinary surgeon.

This book does not dispute that other methods do not always work. They may do in some cases, only that there is another way.

Chapter One:

What do we mean by "Traditional" views?

For many years we were told that dogs needed to be "under control" and that to train them you used a metal choke chain. If they pulled on the lead, lunged towards another dog or showed any aggressive behaviour towards people you were told to snap back hard on the collar and then to release it. The theory behind this surmised that since the collar made a noise, the dog would react and understand that its behaviour was undesirable. However, this was not always the case; the dog did not always stop and did not always understand that its behaviour was undesirable. Instead these dogs associated the punishment with certain situations and would react even more "badly" the next time around. This consequently led to even more choking. Many dogs ended up, and still do, having to be treated for serious neck and back injuries.

Choking is not the only punishment used and there are plenty of other methods such as:
1) **The electric shock collar.**
2) **The rolled up newspaper**.
3) **The stick.**
4) **The citronella spray.**
5) **The shaker.**

Electric Shock Collars

The **electric shock collar** is becoming more and more easily available and is often sold as a "guaranteed" quick fix to stop any unwanted behaviour. The collars administer an electric shock from a remote hand held device and the theory claims the dog will learn to behave as it will receive a shock if it doesn't. But what is the dog really learning? If it gets a shock every time someone approaches the dog may begin to associate people with bad things happening and may try even harder next time to get rid of them. It will not necessarily understand that it is being shocked for showing its teeth since it has performed lots of other behaviours during this time.

The dog may also learn that when it isn't wearing one, it doesn't get hurt and if the occasion arises where the dog is confronted with a person and is not wearing the collar, the situation may become very nasty indeed. You may be getting the dog to do what you want because it **has** to but not because it **wants** to and this is a very important difference to consider.

Many owners who previously used a shock collar also mentioned that once removed it became impossible to get it back on again and that some of their dogs could not get up off the floor with it on as they were shaking so much with fear.

My advice is, if you are thinking of using one on your dog, would you use one on your children?

A shock collar, stick or rolled up newspaper may stop the dog showing aggressive behaviour but this dog is being made not to behave aggressively, it is not learning to stop because it wants to and thus the problem is not being solved.

The thinking behind the citronella collar (a collar that sprays citronella at the dog) and the shaker (a can filled with stones that when shaken makes a loud rattle) is that the dog is distracted away from what it is doing. However, dogs are not stupid and some will quickly learn that if they bark for long enough the spray soon runs out and the noise of the shaker is just a noise and nothing else much happens. They quickly learn to habituate to it (ignore it) and the behaviour continues.

You may believe that you have to make the dog do everything you say. It is human nature to feel embarrassed and cringe when your dog begins to act inappropriately when approached by another human. You feel that you should be able to say the magic word and all will be quiet. However, when this doesn't happen, for whatever reason, you start to get agitated. Not only does the dog pick up on this and react even more badly because they may believe that you too are upset, but the approaching person also becomes anxious. It becomes a catch 22 situation. If an owner shouts at their dog to sit and it doesn't, they may shout louder and then may even resort to pushing its bottom down. But what is the dog learning? It is learning that every time someone approaches the owners gets cross and its bottom gets sore. You also have to ask the question why the owner has to keep shouting louder and louder. Their dog is probably not deaf and can no doubt hear a crisp packet opening three streets away. Is there another way? Can they get their dog to sit because it wants to not because it has to?

The Top Dog view!

A more recent view is that you can get your dog to do anything you wish simply by becoming the "**Top Dog**", "**The Alpha Male**", "**The Leader of the Pack**" by behaving in a "**Dominant**" fashion.

To do this you have to follow a series of "**rules**".

The "rules":

> ➤ Ignore your dog for 5 minutes when you first see it.
> ➤ Make sure you walk up the stairs first.
> ➤ Don't feed your dog if it asks.
> ➤ Eat first.
> ➤ Bark at your dog if it behaves badly.
> ➤ If the behaviour persists drag your dog from the room you are in.
> ➤ Ignore any attempts at interaction by your dog.
> ➤ Don't allow your dog to pull forwards on the lead.

The view is that by becoming "Top Dog, Alpha Male, Leader of the Pack" your dog will listen to you and do as you say. However this theory, based on observations of Wolves in captive situations, relies on the fact that in a natural domestic/feral dog pack there is such thing as a top dog. So is this true? Are dog packs run by one dictator that rules everything the others do? Well **NO** it is not as simple as all that. There are certainly decision makers, healthier, more confident and stronger dogs than others but is there one in particular that rules over all?

Research into domestic/feral dog packs, wolves in the wild and other animals that live in social groups suggests that there probably isn't. It is very dependent on the structure of the group, numbers of individuals, the sex ratio and the situation they find themselves in at the time.

For instance if a healthy, strong male dog who has just eaten a huge meal comes across a starving female who has puppies to feed, and there is a big juicy bone lying between them, which one is going to fight the hardest to get it? Probably the female. However, this doesn't mean she is "Top Dog" over the male. It simply means at this point in time she has more to loose and makes the decision to fight harder for it. He in turn decides it isn't worth the hassle and allows her to take it. In an aggressive encounter with the male in different circumstances it would be more likely that she would defer to him and allow him to take the bone.

When looking at what humans perceive as problem behaviour in dogs it is very important to look very closely at what the dog is doing and understanding why? This needs an extensive knowledge of dog behaviour and is not always as easy to fix as some "views" may suggest.

Dog Behaviour within a familiar group

In dog society it is not the aggressor who decides the winner but the one who knows they can not win and thus defers (looks away and moves off, gives in). Dogs within a pack will have already worked out who they are likely to loose against in an aggressive encounter. After all there is no point in fighting and risking injury every time you meet a familiar face. There would be no dogs left today if they decided to use this type of strategy to decide who gets what. Instead one will defer to the other and conduct their own kind of "doggy manners". They will for instance generally give up their food, mate, den or toy to the winner of these encounters. These "doggy manners" are what we strive to achieve from our dogs during this book. We will stop trying to force our dogs to act like little humans or treat them as if they were under some sort of dictatorship. Domestic dogs are not Wolves just because they are closely related any more than we are Chimpanzees. Although both dogs and Wolves and both humans and Chimps have similarities we all live and behave in very different ways. After all dogs will rip up carpets and jump through hoops to get to us, whereas a wolf will stay as far away from us as possible.

So what can we do if our dogs begin to show behaviour that to us as owners feel is inappropriate? Do we have to resort to violence or behave like a dictator or is there another way to treat our dogs? Yes there is and this book will explain how.

Chapter Two

Choosing the right puppy for you and training it the nice way.

Choosing the right puppy is probably one of the most important decisions you are likely to make. A dog is around for a long time. Therefore, it is essential that that you ask yourself the right questions to find the right dog for you:

- ➢ What sort of environment do I live in? How big is my house, garden and surrounding areas and how many other humans and pets also live here?
- ➢ Can I afford the cost of the puppy, food, bedding, toys, vets fees, training, insurance, grooming and possibly the replacement of damaged items?
- ➢ Have I the time to give my puppy what it needs and am I healthy enough?
- ➢ Where will it spend its time whilst I am away on holiday?
- ➢ How tidy am I? Could I cope with toilet training, shredded toilet roll and endless amounts of dog hair?

Once you are sure you can answer these questions adequately you will then have to ask yourself which type of puppy will be best suited to how you live your life. Obviously a large dog will not be advisable if you live in a small flat with no garden and one that sheds a lot of hair may not be advisable if you are prone to allergies. Likewise if you live a more sedentary life an active dog may not be the dog for you and if you love to walk for miles then a very small dog with short legs may not be what you are looking for either.

There are many breed types and it is a good idea to thoroughly research the ones that interest you and ask many questions. Do not be afraid to approach as many people as possible including your veterinary surgeon, local behaviourist, dog trainers and breeders. You can also visit your library or search the internet. Be aware that choosing the most fashionable breed of the moment may come at a high price and it is possible that the puppies have been bred intensely so may not have had the best start in life.

Once you have decided on a breed, where do you obtain one from? This is a very important part of the choosing process since a puppy's early environment can make a difference to how it turns out in later life. If you have chosen a pedigree, check that the breeder is reputable. Do not be afraid to ask around and visit the breeder before you actually see any of the puppies.

Which puppy to choose?

Choosing which one you like best is often based on how the puppy reacts to you. In most litters of puppies there is often a very bold one, a very nervous one and ones in between. It is very likely that the bolder pup will approach you first but not because it has picked you out for special attention. It's a bold pup and it will approach all new people in the same way. It may be that this one will become a little pushier once it has reached maturity. The cute little one at the back may pull on your heart strings but this may be the one that shows nervous behaviour when older. It is often advisable to choose the middle of the road pup, the one that is a little wary at first but comes happily towards you once you have sat down quietly. However, with the best intentions in the world, sometimes you just have to follow your heart.

How should puppies spend their early life?

The best environment for puppies to grow up in is the one that they will spend their future lives in. Therefore, home bred puppies are more likely to show less behavioural problems than kennel bred ones. However, just because your puppy has been nicely socialised in its early environment does not guarantee you a problem free future just as not all puppies brought up in a barren environment will present you with behavioural problems in the future. However, you will want your puppy to have as good a start in life as possible, therefore, If the puppies are going to be born into a kennel environment ask the breeder how they are going to socialise them and offer to help with the process. If the breeder is agreeable visit the puppies regularly and take along children, adults and other dogs. Pop the puppies in and out of boxes, in and out of the car and take them for very short rides. Pick them up gently and examine them under the ears, belly, mouth and tail. You might be allowed access to a house and a garden where you can get them used to the general noise of home living. If the breeder is not agreeable, question why this may be so!

Rescue Puppies

You may wish to give a home to a puppy from a rescue centre. The same guidelines apply, visit your intended puppy regularly and try to get it used to as many different experiences as possible. Your rescue centre may already have a puppy socialising pen or room set up like a sitting room, where you can spend time with your pup.

The types of experiences you can present are as follows:

➢ Children of differing ages.

➢ Other dogs and pets.

➢ People of a different shapes, sex and sizes wearing a variety of clothing including hat and boots.

➢ Loud noises such as clapping, pots banging and doors slamming. Make sure you begin quietly and as the puppy becomes relaxed with that volume, increase it gradually. There are specialised compact discs (Sounds Scary) that you can use to help your pup cope better with noises such as thunder or fireworks.

➢ Electrical appliances especially the vacuum cleaner.

➢ Being picked up and being examined.

➢ Training sessions of sit and wait.

Ask the staff questions.

➢ Where did the puppy come from and at what age?

➢ If known what are its parents like?

➢ What sort of character it has, i.e. nervous, bold, aggressive or noisy. Does it enjoy a fuss?

➢ How does it get along with its litter mates?

➢ Is it eating well?

➢ Where does it go to the toilet?

By asking lots of questions you will get a better idea of how your puppy may turn out when it is older. I say "may" because even the sweetest of puppies, no matter how good a start they had sometimes turn into the dogs from hell when they start to mature, just like human teenagers. It is very common for adolescence dogs to be given away for re-homing during this stage of their life.

Basic ground-rules and general training the nice way

Once your puppy comes home it is important to lay down some ground rules regarding what it can and can not do and stick to them. Start as you mean to go on. Very often new owners allow their cute little puppy to show behaviours that are not tolerated once the puppy had grown up. Hence the pup gets confused and frustrated and problems may occur.

For instance YES or NO:
1) Are they allowed into the dining area when you are eating?
2) Are they allowed upstairs?
3) Are they allowed up onto the sofa?

Allowing your dog onto the sofa as a special treat only on a Tuesday will only confuse it. Pups do not understand what a special treat is and they definitely do not understand what a Tuesday is. Set yourself some ground rules before you bring the puppy home and make sure the whole family understand why you are doing this.

Dogs on Chairs

Much fuss is made about whether or not you should allow dogs on chairs or beds. In some books it is the 11th commandment, "Thou shalt not allow your dog onto the furniture upon pain of death". My dog has access to both. My reasons are that he prefers to sleep on a chair, he does not shed hair and he looks funny. However, when told to get down he does so with out so much as a grumble. If he were to grumble I would make the decision that he was no longer allowed and take a good look at our relationship. Use your common sense and make an informed decision.

Give your pup a place of its own to hide away in safely, especially at night. Pups often settle better if they are given their own cosy den, such as a crate with a blanket over the top and a basket within. You can also pop in some paper for them to toilet on. However, they will quickly learn not to feel safe in this environment if their owners make this special place a punishment area. Often if a dog misbehaves it is sent to its basket as a punishment. Dogs soon learn to associate the basket with being in trouble and will not feel secure in it. Therefore, allow the basket to become a nice place and not a bad one.

Instead of punishing them by making them sit in their basket, take something away from them instead. If they persistently want your attention take yourself away by ignoring them, if they are trying to snatch a treat or a toy in an inappropriate manner take that away, if they are trying to push themselves through a door, shut it. This leads us nicely onto ways of teaching puppies new instructions.

Puppy training

Sitting

A good way to start training puppies is to ask them to sit before they get anything nice including a treat, dinner, a fuss, verbal praise, lead on, door open or a toy. Puppies can learn this very quickly and all you have to do is show them the reward and wait until they sit back on their bottoms. You can move the treat forwards over their head so they fall back slightly. Once they are sitting repeat the word "sit" is a jolly manner and use the same tone of voice each time. Do not make it a command and shout or push the pup onto its bottom.

Sitting should be associated with a fun instruction, not a punishment; something the pup wants to do, not something it has to. This is where this sort of approach begins to differ from the more traditional approach of dog training. By shouting commands we are in effect punishing our dogs and why punish them for doing something we want them to do? Why punish them for behaving well. But it is surprising how many owners and dog trainers use this sort of approach and make all instructions firm commands. If we were to use this "Victorian" approach towards children today the telephone lines at "Child line" would be red hot. The danger with shouting is that if the dog chooses to ignore your instruction you end up having to shout louder and louder and louder until .... Well then what do you do?

Trying to physically manoeuvre your pup into position will not work either. If you could show dogs how to do things like this you would also be able to teach them to make a pot of tea or put the kids to bed. Obviously this can't happen so why believe you can show them how to sit by this method.

"Learn to Earn"

Teaching your pup to earn its reward.

Once your puppy is sitting (timing is everything) show it the treat and ask it to take it. Once your pup is sitting pretty you can move onto the next stage.

In dog behaviour the lower status dogs defer to the higher status ones by looking and moving their head away. You can achieve this with your puppy by offering the treat asking the pup to **sit.** Once sitting, move the treat closer and if your pup goes to take the reward **without** you giving the instruction remove it quickly whilst saying a firm "**No**". Keep doing this and eventually or quite quickly depending on your pup's character it will stop trying to snatch and will instead blink and look away. Once it is doing this (remember timing is crucial) repeat the word **"wait**" a few times and then tell your pup to "**take it**".

Allow the pup to come to you for the treat. If you move your hand towards it the pup may learn to take its cue from the movement of your hand instead of your voice. When the pup is enjoying the treat use a nice squeaky voice to praise it. The pup will then become conditioned to verbal praise thus in the future you will not always have to use treats as a reward since your voice will be enough.

Once your pup becomes good at this use it as a "learn to earn game", using different rewards in different environments (inside and out). It helps to improve recall, reinforces your status (without the use of direct confrontation), teaches the pup that to get something nice it has to sit down first and thus it is not jumping up all the time. It also helps to teach your pup that when you are displeased nice things disappear and that you actually back up your threat by removing it. If you simply use a cross voice and shout at the pup very soon you will have to shout louder and then louder still. The pup is not deaf but simply leaning that it can ignore you since nothing much happens if it does.

More advance training skills

Once this basic level of training is in place you can then proceed to more advanced levels by asking the pup to wait a little longer before taking the reward. You can incorporate this instruction during the wait phase of the "learn to earn game". Ask the pup to sit and during the wait take a few steps back and then forwards again. At other times you can place the reward onto the floor. You can then teach your pup to lie down by rewarding and repeating the instruction whilst the pup is lying down. Therefore, you are teaching your pup to wait and it will willingly since it is learning that nice things happen if it waits. This is a much nicer way than forcing your pup to wait by punishing it if it doesn't.

Forcing the issue does not work and is not a quick fix:

 ➤ Pushing your puppy down into a sit will only teach your pup that to get a reward it has to be physically pushed down by you first.
 ➤ Pulling your puppy back on the lead to stop it pulling will only teach it that to get to go forwards it has to be pulled back first.

The Importance of Timing

Timing as I stated earlier is very important, dogs live in the here and now. I often see owners shouting at their dog for not coming back after the dog has actually come back. If you tell your dog off for not coming back when it is sitting in front of you, how on earth is it supposed to understand that you are displeased at something it did or didn't do two minutes ago! All it will understand is that it is being shouted at for what it is doing at that precise time and that is standing in front of its owner. Confusing for the dog? I should say so. Dogs live in the here and now and timing is crucial hence you say "no" whilst you are taking the treat away not before and not after. Therefore, "no" becomes your punishment word and will help you and your pup to understand each other better when it comes to your puppy doing things you do not want it to. For instance it may want to chew your shoe, you say "no" firmly take it away and then give your pup something it can chew on after it has sat and waited for it.

You can not show dogs what to do and expect them to understand what it is you expect from them. They do not copy your actions or understand long complicate sentences. What they are good at is putting two and two together. If jumping up makes you react to them, they will jump. If sitting looking at you whilst you are eating gets them a bit of sausage, they will beg and if barking at you makes you tell them to shut up, they will bark. Just because you don't see being told off as a reward doesn't mean your pup won't.

As with small children often any attention is good attention.

Any attention is good attention

A prime example of this was illustrated by my little girl Chloe when she was two years old. Whenever I was talking to a client on the phone she would begin to try and get my attention away from the phone and back onto her. Initially she would simply try to talk to me, after these attempts were ignored with the help of a cordless phone; she tried to give me a book or a pretend cup of tea. This still didn't gain an effect so she showed her true colours and resorted to banging things about in her room. I thought I had won this by totally ignoring her at all times until that one fateful day when the phone rang whilst Chloe was on the toilet. As I was speaking professionally to a client I heard the plaintiff cry of "MUMMY I HAVE DONE A DIRTY POO". I was in a fix. Do I ignore her and face consequences of having to buy a new carpet or do I react and face a lifetime of plaintiff cries. I had to react after all I was a mum and new carpets are expensive. Therefore, every time the phone rang, I would here the patter of tiny footsteps up the stairs to the toilet followed by that plaintiff cry. She hadn't planned this clever approach, she wasn't old enough, she just happened to be on the loo when the phone rang and it worked for her so she did it over and over again. How she managed to produce so much poo each time I will never know.

Dogs don't plan either but it often looks like they do and I have come across some amazing attention seeking behaviours during my work. One dog, a Spaniel, called Lucy had learned to howl in a high pitched squeal whenever her owner was not giving her enough attention. It was so loud and she persisted for so long that the owner and her vet believed that something very odd was going on and a lot of money was spent on specialists, scans and tests. The owner would try to shut Lucy up by telling her to "be quiet!" and was of course reinforcing the howling by doing so. And anyway how does a dog know what "shut up" actually means? It may be aware of you becoming cross but shutting up is a complicated concept to learn. In the end when all else had failed she approached me and I recommended (amongst other things) that she ignore all Lucy's attempts at soliciting attention but to reward her by giving it back once the howling had stopped. It took two days, a very detailed behavioural modification programme and some ear plugs. Then all was quiet again.

We will keep returning to the concept of getting your dog to do something it wants to rather than has to. In the case described previously trying to shut Lucy up by force would not have worked simply because for Lucy any attention was good attention. The owner could have used fiercer methods of getting her to shut up such as a spray of citronella to the face or a shock collar. However, this would not have addressed the question as to why Lucy needed her owner's attention so badly in the first place. Acting as the "top dog" and ignoring Lucy would not have addressed her problems either since she needed lots of attention but of the right sort. Simply ignoring her would have made Lucy feel very distressed.

Other aspects of owning a puppy.

1) Toilet training how long does it take?

How long is a piece of a string? Toilet training depends on your puppy abilities to learn, the environment it lives in and how much time you have available to pursue this. It's a bit like potty training some children take longer than others and every frustrated mother knows that at least half the other children in nursery have been dry for months. Remain patient and do not try and force the issue by punishing your puppy for not getting on with it. Likewise showing them a video of other puppies peeing appropriately will not do the trick either.

Puppies learn to associate different substrates with the pleasant release of emptying the bladder or bowls. You do not even need to reward them for going as going itself is a reward. Therefore, when its time for a tinkle, pop your puppy onto the substrate of your choice. The more often they go on a particular substrate the quicker they will associate using this area. Pop them out at regular intervals especially after meals, first thing in the morning and last thing at night. If you see them about to go in the house firmly say "no" and remove them to a more appropriate place. Do not punish them for using the wrong place after they have already done it and especially **do not rub their noses in it.** Dogs are clever but not that clever! They are not going to be able to understand what it is you are trying to show them and this may cause them to go when you are not looking.

2) What to do and what to chew?

Puppies should not chew shoes, TV remotes, table legs, Lego or anything small that can be easily swallowed. There are many commercially available toys that are designed to be chewed and puzzled over. I love the types of toys that ask your dog to work hard to gain the treat. It gives them something to do that is mentally stimulating and rewarding. I often advise that owners feed their dogs using these toys. After all in the wild, food does not come in small plastic bowls, dogs have to work very hard to gain it and thus have time allotted to this activity in their natural doggy timetable.

3) How to play?

Toys that encourage **tug of war** should be avoided if your puppy begins to get overly excited or does not let go when you ask it to. Unfortunately this is often fraught with difficulty since many types of dogs love tuggy games as do most husbands. Play throwing or hiding games instead and always allow the pup to take the toy from you only after it has sat and waited (learn to earn game) as described earlier. Although you may believe your pup is only "playing", these games are all part of learning what it can and can not get away with. Puppies do not stay puppies for long! The same goes with **"mouthing"** if your puppy starts to mouth you say "no" remove your arm/leg/pocket and stop the game by walking away. If they are hanging onto your trousers or skirt, unzip and walk out of them. But do remember to close the curtains.

When playing **rough and tumble,** another game enjoyed by dog and husband, think about what it is you are teaching your puppy! By coming down to its level you are deferring and by initiating contact sports you are challenging it. It can all get a bit confusing for the pup. Therefore, make it clear what types of play are appropriate for your pup at an early age.

If your puppy plays the "**look what I have got and you are not having it because I can run away faster than you"** game do not succumb. Instead pick up something else more interesting, turn your back and become interested in that toy, the now first prize. The toy your pup has will soon loose its appeal since you are no longer interested in it. It will promptly drop this and come up to you wanting what you have. Pick up the dropped toy and you can ask pup to sit and wait before getting the new one. What has happened is that by remaining calm, and using your brain you have managed to retrieve the toy or it may have been the remote control or the latest mobile phone without any undue hassle or by force. The pup has dropped it because it chose to do so not because it had to and you still reinforced your status since the pup had to sit, defer and wait before getting the new one.

To help stop the novelty from wearing off you can rotate the toys weekly and to make them even more interesting add a little bit of the outside dirt onto them.

4) Puppy's social calendar?

You may be told that to socialise your puppy to other dogs you must attend a regular course of puppy parties. Organised in an appropriate way these can be of great value to you and your new pup. However, by the time your puppy has had all its vaccinations the window of opportunity for socialising has closed and thus in this context too late. This biologically pre-programmed sensitive period in early life occurs from birth to around 14 weeks of age depending on breed type. During this period exposure to experiences and situations have a greater effect on later development. However, this doesn't mean your puppy will not learn anything. On the contrary organised in the right way these parties can help teach your puppy how to show appropriate behaviour with other puppies and adult dogs, humans and children and if they are held at a veterinary centre they teach your puppy that these places are actually nice places to visit. What they should **not** be is a free for all where the puppies may learn how to fight and that other dogs are so much fun that in later life they may show inappropriate over-excited behaviour when meeting one. There are some very well organised parties around the country and I have included an address at the end of this book to help you find one in your local area.

5) Taking the lead.

The first time on the lead can be a harrowing experience for a young puppy especially if it is pulled around the floor by its neck. Begin by using a soft collar and lead and allow your puppy to wander around the garden with it on. Do not pull at it or try to force your pup to follow you. Just calmly follow it around and then call the pup to you and reward with a small treat. Once your pup is used to having the lead on you can start to walk further a field. Begin by carrying it a short distance from your house, allow it to sniff around and gently encourage it back. With each journey move a little further and further away until your pup begins to trot quite happily back on the nice loose lead. If it stops and pulls back do not yank it forwards, just stand there and calmly call the pup towards you and wait. If the area is safe you can even drop the lead and begin to walk away. Get your puppy used to walking on a loose lead and contrary to belief there is not an 11th commandment stating "Thou shalt have your dog walking to heal by your leg whilst looking directly up at you at all times and he shall absolutely not sniff at lampposts."

Unless you intend to train your puppy in obedience for Crufts, walking alongside quietly and having the odd sniff at a lamppost is a much more fun than being frogmarched around the block stuck to the side of your owner's leg. Most breeds of dog are not cut out for this type of intense training anyway and will never make the mark even if you wanted them to. Walking should be a fun and pleasant experience for all not a military procedure. I would rather see a happy and content dog interested in its environment than one walking "perfectly" to heel looking miserable.

Pee-mail

Sniffing at lampposts, trees, bushes and every clump of grass is a normal part of dog behaviour and the smells they omit are full of useful doggy information to be mulled over. For your puppy going for a walk where other dogs have been is like walking in a world full of post it notes from hundreds of interesting characters which are there to be read and digested.

Dogs read and send pee-mails all the time and this helps to mentally stimulate them. Mental stimulation is as important as the physical aspect and should not be frowned at.

Chapter Three

Aggression just what is it and why does my dog behave this way?

Problems regarding aggression are amongst the most common problems dealt with by behaviourists and the largest killer of dogs in the UK, Europe and the USA. There is still the old adage that once a dog has tasted blood there is nothing you can do but put the dog to sleep, hence the hasty death of thousands of dogs. However, it is a lot more complicated than that. There are many reasons why dogs show aggression and many different forms of aggressive behaviour.

What does the word aggression mean to us?

If we look in the dictionary it describes aggression as "an unprovoked attack" and "hostile activity". Stick aggression into your computers thesaurus and words such as "violence, anger, assault" and "injury" appear. All very emotive expressions, but what do we know about dog aggression? Is what we think we are seeing genuinely unprovoked violent anger?

What does aggression mean to dogs?

Why do dogs show aggressive behaviour in the first place? Well we all know that they can bite their owners, other dogs and strangers, but why?

The answer to this depends on the situation they find themselves in:

➤ A dog may have learned that behaving aggressively gets it a valued resource.

➤ A dog may have formed a negative association with a particular situation and is defending itself.

➤ It may be frightened and is behaving aggressively to save itself.

➤ A female with puppies may be protecting them from what she perceives as harm.

➤ A dog may be in pain and is trying to stop it getting worse.

➤ A dog may have learned that fighting over food is the only way it gets any.

➤ Two dogs that live together may be competing for a valued resource such as bone or the attention of their owner.

➤ A dog might be meeting an unfamiliar dog for the first time and both may threaten and challenge each other.

➤ A dog may be defending itself or its territory from what it feels is a threat.

➤ It may be a breed type that has been designed to react aggressively towards other dogs.

➤ It may be a dog that has been bred to show high predatory behaviour.

➤ It may even be that the dog has been trained to show aggressive behaviour.

Some of these aggressive behaviours are quite normal or understandable, some may be out of context and therefore inappropriate and in some cases the aggressive behaviour is not normal at all. Thus there are many reasons why a dog may show aggressive behaviour and it is very important that you understand the reasons behind it and seek help from a qualified companion animal behaviourist.

Do not try any attempt to correct this behaviour by a "do it yourself" method. The use of punishment or behaving as if you were "top dog" may result in disaster.

Body language

Dogs do not only show aggression by biting and growling at each other. One of the ways dogs communicate how they are feeling is by using body language. They exhibit a number of behaviours and postures many of which we are still yet to learn. By using different postures they can indicate to each other that if they were to fight, who the likely winner of this is going to be.

Fighting every dog you meet is not a good strategy for survival, even if you did win most of the time, since it is likely that you would still gain an injury. Since there are few vets living behind bushes waiting to leap out with syringes full of antibiotics even a small cut could result in loss of fitness or even death.

By showing each other their strengths they can make an informed decision whether to defer or not, in other words give in.

These postures communicate lots of different meanings to other dogs:
- Whether they are willingly to interact for example by wagging their tail.
- How big they are, by making themselves look larger and having the hairs on their body stick up.
- How much armour they possess by presenting the other dog with a row of shiny white teeth. Teeth also show how young and fit you are.

- ➢ How healthy they are by being able to bark and growl loudly and for a very long time. It's hard work shouting loudly for a long time.
- ➢ How strong they are by bowling another dog over and squeezing the back of its neck with its jaws. Some dogs even use mounting behaviour.
- ➢ How much mental strength they have by holding eye contact and not backing down.

Being able to show each other your physical strengths is a great indicator of who is likely to win a fight. However, I hear you all cry, "I've got a Jack Russell Terrier and he stands up to Rottweiler's". Well physical strength is only part of it, mental strength, the self belief that you are going to win or even the desperation that you have to, is just as important. Some dogs and some breed types have more "mental strength" than others and will win a battle of wills over much bigger dogs. Mental strengths include holding eye contact with another dog without blinking and having the audacity to even try in the first place.

Once a dog has decided the likely outcome of having a fight and what they have to gain from it, they can either increase the aggression to involve more serious behaviours such as actually biting or they can stop the fight by deferring.

These deference postures are often the opposite of aggressive challenging ones:
- ➢ Instead of becoming big and threatening a dog will become small by lowering its body and hiding away the ears and tails.
- ➢ They take all eye contact away and may move away.
- ➢ They give up all possessions to the victor.

Usually this is enough and the victor may mark his success with a little urine and wander off or invite a non-challenging interaction. However, not all dogs, for whatever reason, seem to understand this behaviour and continue to challenge after the other dog has deferred. This is a form of inappropriate aggressive behaviour.

In these cases the deferring dog may:
- ➢ Try to escape.
- ➢ Show even more deferent posturing by clamping its tail firmly between its legs and flattening its body to the ground.
- ➢ Roll over and sometimes even urinate. Some dogs show this form of fearful deference when another dog or human simply looks at them.
- ➢ Others may react to a continuous challenge by becoming defensive and reacting in an aggressive way even though their initial response was to defer.

There is a fine line between normal deference and really fearful posturing and like people all dogs have a slightly different genetic makeup and have experienced slightly different environments and will show varying extremes of this.

Like people all dogs are different but some are more different than others.

To help illustrate how complicated aggressive issues are, I will describe two case histories both with similar presenting signs. Both dogs were aggressive towards people they did not know, but both had completely different reasons why they showed this behaviour. Let's first meet a dog called "Molly".

Molly's story.

Molly was an 18 month-old Border Collie who was obtained from a farm in South Yorkshire. The farmer had advertised the puppies in a local newspaper stating that they would make "great and intelligent pets". She was born in a barn on the farm and had five other brothers and sisters. Her mother was a working farm Collie and her father was also a working dog from another farm and although the owners saw the mother they did not see the father. They described the mothers character as very nervous but not aggressive and she did not want to interact with them. However, the puppies looked cute especially the one who cowered behind her mother at the back of the box. Being human they picked this pup to take home. Molly was 6 weeks old. She spent her first few weeks hiding behind the sofa but eventually came around and became quite happy in the company of her owners and their two young children.

The owners led a quiet life and did not have many people visit the house. If they did, Molly would keep away from them and hide. When she was 9 months old the owners decided that Molly should attend "obedience classes". The sort of classes she went to used a more "traditional" approach and recommended that all dogs wore a choke chain and collar. Molly was not used to one of these and began to pull away from it. The "dog trainer" saw this and told the owners to be a lot firmer with her and showed them how to pull back and release the chain. He only got to demonstrate this once as the second time Molly decided that enough was enough and began to growl as he approached her. The dog trainer became very angry, grabbed the lead from the owners and pulled hard. Molly reaction was to cry and lay flat on the floor. The trainer was about to repeat this when the owners stepped in to stop him, they left and didn't return. All was well for a few months until Molly began to mature and her nervous behaviour worsened. Instead of hiding when people arrived at the house she began to sit in between them and her owners and if the visitors made a sudden move she would bare her teeth and growl. Her owners understandably started to worry and put her out of the room whenever anyone came to the house. As soon as the door bell rang, Molly was frantically bundled into the kitchen.

It came to a head one day when a visitor tried to approach and stroke Molly whilst she was in the kitchen. This person informed the owners that she had endless years of dog experience and "knew how to handle dogs"! Molly not knowing this promptly bit her and the person told the owners that Molly was beyond help and would have to be put down. The owners were distraught and asked their vet for help who referred her to me.

When I entered the house on the first consultation it was clear that Molly was scared to death of me. Her body carriage was low with her ears flat and tail clamped tightly beneath her legs. She stared hard at me and curled her lips. I did not challenge by look directly at her and ignored her completely. We had a nice cup of tea, some biscuits and chatted about Molly and general dog behaviour. Eventually, after an hour or so Molly came closer and seemed a little more relaxed. Her body carriage was still low but she had stopped curling her lips and her ears were pricked up. I still ignored her and waited for her to wander away. I then called her over calmly and produced a tasty treat from my bag. Without looking directly at her I offered her the treat but asked her to sit and wait first using the "learn to earn" exercise described earlier in the book. She came and willingly sat and waited for the treat. I did not look directly at Molly since she may have viewed this as challenging. Instead I allowed her to gain enough confidence to approach in her own time. However, by asking her to defer to me first before receiving the treat I was also saying indirectly that I was the stronger animal. She understood this body language and her *confidence grew as she learned that I was not going to make a grab for her. After the consultation she had become a lot more relaxed in my presence.*

Molly had <u>not</u> been showing the previous visitor, whom she had bitten, that she was the "Top dog". She was simply reacting in a defensive manner and had tried to tell this person, in the only way she could, not to approach as she was frightened by what this person might do to her. However, this person had not understood Molly's body language and all Molly could do was to carry out her threat to bite.

Common approach to greeting a dog

Many people still approach a dog by staring at it and showing a whole row of teeth (we call it smiling). We then make loud cooing noises, bend over it and go for the back of the neck. This is what dogs do to each other when they are challenging one another. It is little wonder that some people get bitten when they approach a dog in this way. Luckily most dogs learn that we do not mean anything by this gesture and will ignore it and some may even enjoy the feeling. But some, especially if they feel threatened, may view this approach very differently. If you are meeting an unfamiliar dog for the first time, do not stare at it or attempt contact, just ignore it. The dog will feel a lot happier with this non-challenging approach.

It is not being rude. Being rude is purely a human concept.

Why Molly behaved in this way was understandable if we look at her breed type and early learning experiences. Farm Collies have been designed by years of breeding programmes to show an instinctive predatory response to herding farm animals. This instinctive response is thought to be genetically linked with nervous/aggressive behaviour and many farm collies show defensive behaviour towards any animals/humans they find threatening. Molly's mother also showed nervous behaviour towards unfamiliar people. Farm Collies are also generally born outside the home environment and may not have had a great deal of early experience with different people. This may result with them having difficulties coping with new people in later life.

Molly's experience with the "dog trainer" would not have helped and may have left her with a very negative experience from which to refer to. Alongside all these reasons her owners may have also helped to reinforce her negative experiences by becoming distressed every time the door bell rang and bundling Molly into the kitchen.

For problems with this much complexity there is no such thing as a quick fix or an instant cure. In most behavioural cases there are many factors to consider and we hope that the owners are able to manage the problem safely and go some way in achieving positive results. Any owner expecting a perfect new and improved dog over night is going to be disappointed and will probably resort to the promises of quick fixes from some drug companies or electric collar manufacturers. In Molly's case it was important that she was never allowed to be put into a situation where she could bite again, defensively or not. Her owners were advised not to react anxiously but to make sure that the visitors were not allowed to approach Molly and that she either wore a muzzle, was on a house line or chewing on something tasty in the kitchen.

Muzzles?

Muzzling can be a useful accessory once the dog gets used to it. However, you must make sure that it is the right size for your dog. It is also important that the dog associates it with nice things rather than having it shoved on when ever another person approaches. Therefore, pop it on and off on a regular basis during the wait period of the learn to earn game.

Not only does a muzzle protect other people and gives peace of mind to the owners but is a great deterrent in stopping other people trying to stroke your dog and thus frightening it.

It was also just as important to teach Molly that visitors were actually quite nice things to have around and a behavioural programme was designed in which Molly was asked to play a "learn to earn game" at a distance where she could see a person but they were not so close that she would react nervously. Over time the distance she could cope was shortened and eventually she was able to walk past people more confidently and allow people in the house without reacting aggressively. She will never be a bold and friendly dog since we can't give her a genetic transplant nor recreate her early learning experiences but we could help to teach her that people were not as scary as she once believed. Her owners will always have to be aware of placing her into situations she can't cope with but she is a lot calmer and hasn't bitten anyone since.

Bruce's Story:

The next case I want to talk about is another dog that had bitten a visitor but for very different reasons. This is Bruce's story.

Bruce was a long haired male German Shepherd of 18 months who like Molly was approaching maturity. They owners bought him from a breeder who showed German Shepherds and all the puppies were brought up in a home environment. The owners picked Bruce out of the litter because he immediately bound up and seemed to choose them. He was the biggest and boldest puppy and full of life. Bruce was taken to his new home at 12 weeks of age and was soon bouncing around and chewing everything in sight.

He was taken to "obedience classes" where the trainers only used positive reward methods. Bruce found it great fun and approached all the other puppies and bowled them over. He became quite a character and this behaviour was tolerated as his behaviour was described as "playful". He soon learned all the commands and was soon walking to heal, sitting, lying down and coming when called with joyous enthusiasm during these classes.

However, at home his behaviour was not always as good, he did not always sit and he did not always come when called. He would also constantly present his owners with toys to throw for him and the more his owners tried to tell him to go away the more toys he bought. If they tried to take the toy from him he would run away hanging on to it for dear life. He could apparently keep this game up all evening and would remain active at most times during the day and constantly paced around the room and the garden. He had also started to follow his female owner everywhere even when she went to the loo.

At first they thought this behaviour was funny and it was not until a family friend came to visit that they suddenly realised that they had a big problem on their hands. This particular family male friend was a regular visitor and had known Bruce since he was a puppy. They had always got on well and often played rough and tumble, a common pursuit particularly among the males of both species. However, on this particular visit Bruce was sitting between this friend and his female owner. The family friend just happened to lean over to give the female owner a letter he had received when Bruce suddenly leapt up and grabbed his arm. This was a particularly nasty grab and left the friend with 12 stitches. The owners rushed Bruce to their vets the very next day with the intention of having him put to sleep. The forward thinking veterinary surgeon took a detailed history regarding Bruce's early life, his character and the events of the previous night. He noticed that there may be a problem with status and protective issues and asked if the owners would be willingly to speak to me first. They did and Bruce is still alive to day albeit minus his manhood, a small price to pay.

Although the end result was the same in both Molly's and Bruce's case, that two people were bitten within the family home, the factors underlying them were completely different and each needed a different approach. Bruce was an intact maturing male show-bred German Shepherd dog and was the boldest puppy in the litter. In all probability Bruce did not choose his owners when he was a puppy, he would have reacted in exactly the same way towards anyone that came to see him. He grew into a big strong dog and learned all the usual "commands" needed to become the "perfect dog". However, just because he knew the commands, didn't mean he was going to carry them out. Instead he began to show selective hearing. He also learned that he could initiate contact when he liked and someone would react to him. He "played" rough and tumble games which he *often won and kept his female owner under close scrutiny at all times. In other words the humans around him would defer to his requests for resources and he emerged the victor.*

So why if he got all he wanted would he have reacted aggressively toward the male visitor? Well probably for several reasons, although we can't actually ask Bruce or get inside his head to experience it for ourselves.

1) Bruce was bred from show stock to obtain a breed standard asked for by the Kennel Club. Initially German Shepherds had been bred as territory guarding dogs, not show dogs, and these guard dogs often show a more nervous character and hence find a lot of things threatening so may react in a defensive manner. However, show dogs have not been bred for their guarding skills, since a nervous dog is more likely to react defensively when poked and prodded by the judge and will not to present itself very well in front of unfamiliar people. Hence Bruce may be genetically pre-disposed to behave in a much bolder way.

2) Bruce had been given lots of attention by his owners whenever he asked for it. Therefore, his owners may have become an important resource for him to compete over. This deferring behaviour by the owners may have also increased his concept of where he belonged in the group.

3) Bruce was also beginning to mature into a fully fledged male dog with increasing amounts of sexual hormones being released. It is possible that Bruce may have viewed his female owner as an important mating resource and he was competing with the male friend.

4) It may have been that the male friend startled him by suddenly reaching out over the top and thus he reacted quickly in a defensive manner.

It may have been partly, all or none of these factors. It was my belief, after taking a full history that Bruce was showing behaviour more akin to competitive behaviour and was viewing his owners (especially his female owner) as very important resources. It was, therefore, important that these status issues were addressed and Bruce was no longer given attention on demand.

His behavioural modification programme included such recommendations as:

i. It was important that visitors to the house were safe; therefore Bruce was either kept calmly on a house line or had his muzzle on. All visitors were asked not to look, touch, talk or to approach him. However, Bruce was rewarded with treats or attention by his owners when he was calm. This enabled him to begin to associate having visitors around with nice things happening to him.

ii. To help him become less competitive his owners had to make sure that he learned to earn all his rewards and that he deferred to them first. They no longer gave in to his demands for attention and were very clear and consistent in their instructions.

iii. However, ignoring your dog is a miserable way to live for both parties since dogs are social creatures and have needs, so the owners were encouraged to play and interact with him but in a more appropriate way. There were no more games of rough and tumble but more instead of hide, throw and fetch.

iv. To keep him amused he was given puzzle games which consisted of toys in which the owners could place a small treat. He was also given raw hide chews and a Kong with a small smearing of fish paste inside.

v.   *He was also given two good quality walks daily where he was allowed to run and sniff and play the "learn to earn" game described earlier in the book.*

vi.   *He was also neutered since this is known to reduce competitive aggression by reducing the amount of the hormone testosterone. This hormone produced in the testes makes the dog likely to fight more often and for longer than those dogs that have had their testes removed. And of course this will also help to stop any unwanted mini Bruce's and Sheila's running around.*

Since he no longer views his owners' as such important resources he does not show any of the competitive aggressive behaviours. However, at times he still tries to challenge his owners by thrusting the odd squeaky bone into their laps and they have to remember to ignore this behaviour. Theirs is a life changing programme and because of his naturally bold nature the owners will always have to keep a lid on status issues.

DOMINANCE

I do not like to use the word dominance, as it conjures up all sorts of meanings for different people. Scantily clad ladies with high leather boots carrying whips and chains springs to my mind when I hear the word dominance? "To dominate" is described in the Collins Gem dictionary as to "rule, control, sway, and be the most powerful". If you stick this word in your computer thesaurus you get similar results and words like "govern, dictate, take over". Was Bruce really viewing his owners in this way and thinking up new ways to dictate to them his wishes? Probably not, dogs just don't have the type of brain structure to be able to think like this. He was certainly challenging them for status but dominating is far too an emotive word to use and gives the wrong impression.

Therefore, I prefer to use the phrase "status issues" and think of the dog as showing its strengths rather than trying to dominate.

Status issues

In doggy world, if the owner is deferring to their dog by giving in to constant demands for attention then the dog will expect the rewards that come with that status. Of course in natural dog groups changes in status occur at regular intervals as new dogs mature and old dogs become weak and ill. Being higher in status allows access to rewards over those of lower status such as mating opportunities, a drink of water, sleeping areas or food.

However, there is not one ruling dictator that rules above the rest. Dog society is a lot more fluid than that and is very dependent on how they are feeling at that time. For instance, some dogs' covert food over sleeping areas and are more likely to fight harder for a meal than a bed in one instance but may change their minds if they are particularly cold one night. Female dogs seem more willingly to fight harder over resources that involve bringing up puppies, such as food and den areas, whereas the males tend to fight harder over mating opportunities with females. Some dogs become very possessive over attention and will not allow another dog or human anywhere near their precious owner.

As I have mentioned earlier, fighting at all times is not a very good strategy since the victors may also become injured. Instead dogs will use behavioural postures to show their strengths until one decides to defer. However, some authors have picked up on the "dominance" aspect only and have described methods of training using only this small part of dog behaviour and use it subsequently to cover all problem behaviour. This they claim is all you have to do to get your dog to behave appropriately.

Others go even further than this approach by asking the owners to physically fight their dogs by scruffing them by the neck and wrestling them to the ground or by taking their food away from them. "So what's wrong with that then I hear you cry", well for one thing it assumes that this is what actually happens in dog society, that there is only the one leader. It also assumes that the dog can actually understand what it is you are trying to say. In both cases the assumption is misleading and used inappropriately these approaches can be damaging since they do not take into account the nervous, overly bold or those dogs that have not been successful in learning normal dog behaviour.

So is there another way of addressing status issues that is less challenging to your dog?

Yes, instead of trying to force the issue you could ask your dog to defer to you in a non-confrontational way. In other words stay in control by not having to fight them in a one to one battle. I have already described "**the learn to earn"** exercise earlier in the book and described how you can cleverly retrieve the remote controls, mobile phones and your best underwear by using your more complicated problem solving brains.

The idea behind the more non-confrontational approach is that we use the dogs own "doggy manners" to try keep our dogs within appropriate behavioural boundaries. However, trying to emulate being a dog is pretty difficult since we have no clear understanding of how dogs think or really view the world but we can try with what available evidence we already have. Fortunately today we have a much better understanding of how dogs behave, a clearer picture of their anatomy and physiology and how they learn.

How dogs learn to associate

This area is a book in its own right so instead of realms of text I will try and describe how dogs learn by discussing a situation most of us as dog owners will be familiar with.

JUMPING UP

When a dog first greets you it can be a joyous affair, you encourage your dog by smiling, talking to it and giving it a big fuss. Then you get a bit cross because your dog is beginning to snag your new pure lambs-wool designer cardigan so you start reacting in a totally different way. The dog picks up on your body language and tone of voice and understands that you are not so happy. Therefore, it tries to please you more by jumping even higher after all that worked in the first place. By now you are really cross and the dog gets a serious telling off and probably a sore nose. Poor dog it has only shown you one behaviour, which, at first you rewarded and then you didn't. How is a dog supposed to understand that it can only jump up at you for 6.8 seconds and only on those days when you are not wearing a new lambs-wool cardigan? The answer is it can't. Jumping up worked the first time so the dog will continue to jump up and the more excited you get the higher it will jump.

So what's the answer?

This is very easy you have to do is to say "No" and firmly ignore (no eye, voice or body contact) it by turning away. Eventually if it is not getting rewarded for jumping it will stop. Then you can reward it when it has its bottom planted firmly on the ground.

It has not stopped because it suddenly sees you as the leader dog and dogs do not jump up at leader dogs.

It has stopped because it has learned that jumping does not get it the reward it wanted, however, sitting on its bottom does!

Chapter Four.

Aggressive behaviour towards other dogs.

We all have this idyllic picture of long balmy walks, meeting other owners and seeing our dogs frolicking joyfully together amongst the tall grass. However, life isn't always like that and for some owners walking the dog has become their worse nightmare. Meeting another dog can often mean having to desperately hang on to your dog whilst it throws itself into a frenzy of pulling, barking and frothing at the mouth. Or having to walk at unseemly hours of the day and night and in places you would never normally go. This is not a pleasant experience for dog or owner and life can become very stressful and complicated. So why is this such a common occurrence? Why do some dogs act this way when confronted with another of their own species?

Well there are as usual many different reasons why this may happen. A common and much over used explanation is that the dog was not socialised as a young puppy and didn't receive enough contact with other types of dog. However, there are plenty of dogs out there who were and they still behave this way so what else may be occurring? To give us a clearer picture it's important to look at how dogs behave naturally towards intruder dogs without our "help" and intervention.

Territory behaviour in wild groups

In the wild domestic/feral dogs live in groups and defend the territory in which they live. In this territory there will be food, dens, water and also females who are very important if you are a male dog. Each member of the group is familiar with each other and have already worked out who defers (backs down) to whom and when. However, when an unfamiliar dog approaches he or she will have to be investigated and decisions made regarding whether this dog is allowed to stay within the group or not. If so the whole process of who defers to whom and when will have to be established all over again. If a large group of dogs approach intending to take over the territory then world war three will probably take place. Therefore, it is quite normal for dogs to want to suss each other out and they do this by smell, body posture and often challenging behaviours to gauge each others intentions.

However, our domestic dogs do not generally live in the wild and have to adapt to living within groups consisting of humans and often other species of animals. They may not have an established territory outside of the home area as they are walked in different areas and they will often meet a much higher density of other dogs than they would normally in the wild. Domestic dogs have also been bred over hundreds of years by humans to fulfil a particular purpose and may not always react to situations as a wild domestic/feral dog might.

Generally when unfamiliar domestic dogs meet:
- They may challenge each other, by adopting a stiffened body posture.
- They may show each other their teeth or make a lot of noise
- They may stare at each other unblinkingly.

- ➤ They may attempt to sniff each other; usually around areas we may perceive to be unsociable.
- ➤ They may try to place their body or jaws over the back of each other.
- ➤ They may try to bowl the other dog over or even mount them.
- ➤ They may stiffen and turn their heads away in a non-confrontational way.
- ➤ They may simply ignore the other dog.
- ➤ Some show extreme deference and even fearful behaviour towards oncoming dogs.
- ➤ Some bounce up and down with their bottoms in the air and with their front legs straight. This is known as a play bow and the dogs are telling each other that they want to chase and run about without challenging.

These postures and behaviours all form part of the body language developed by nature to communicate intentions. How willing they are to fight or to defer, how strong and whether they would be able to win a fight if one occurred. Normally at this point one dog will make the decision to defer by backing down and looking away. The victor will accept this and the behaviours cease.

All these behaviours are quite normal and what dogs do.

However, some owners do <u>not</u> like their dogs to do this and view these behaviours as **undesirable.** After all their dogs should be behaving perfectly and perfect dogs do everything their owners tell them to do. They certainly should not be acting in this unruly manner. After all if another human greeted everyone they met by sniffing crotches and trying to mount them they would soon be up in front of the magistrate's court.

But we must <u>not</u> treat our dogs as if they were human, they are not, they are dogs with their own highly developed language. Often when we try to force our own rules and regulations upon them things go horribly wrong.

Human intervention

Off course not all dogs act how they would naturally when meeting other dogs. They have had a little help from their so called best friends. Over centuries humans have bred dogs for their different abilities:

➤ Some dogs have been bred for their fighting prowess and have been designed to fight other dogs.

➤ Others may have been bred for their predatory ability to herd or hunt and have an urge to chase anything that runs.

➤ Some are simply stuck in puppy mode and want to play and can feel very frustrated if they are stopped from doing this.

There are plenty of other factors involved such as:

➤ Wanting to protect their owners from what they see as a threat, which is often reinforced by the owner reacting in a stressful way.

➤ Some dogs are simply frightened of approaching dogs for whatever reason.

➤ Others become worse when they hit their teenage years or become Victor Meldrews when they hit pension age.

➤ Some male dogs only react to other male dogs.

➤ Some female dogs only react to female dogs.

> ➢ Some dogs only react to larger ones or of a particular colour.

There are many different factors underlying this problem. What the dog is probably **NOT** doing is being naughty and rude just to annoy or to dominate us. However, it is constantly learning from this experience and what it learns depends again on many different factors.

What your dog may be learning

So let's go back to our struggling owner hanging on for grim death to their frenzied dog. There they are frantically struggling, becoming more and more stressed and embarrassed at what the other owner must think of them. Their arms feel like they are being pulled out of their sockets and their voice horse with trying to shout instructions to their dog over the cacophony of barking and choking noises. So what is this situation actually teaching the dog?

Well one obvious consideration springs to mind in that every time this dog sees another dog, bad things happen, not only to it but to the owners as well. This is an important point to consider. This dog will not necessarily understand that the owner is stressed due to its behaviour or what it might do in the next few seconds. Only that every time another dog approaches all hell breaks loose. And why should it. after all it's a dog living in the here and now. It is an animal that is totally brilliant at identifying smells, but rubbish at planning ahead and completing crossword puzzles. It has no concept of human right or wrong. It simply associates approaching dogs with bad things happening to it so reacts by trying to get rid of the threat. The owner by shouting and pulling is continuingly reinforcing this behaviour and the whole process becomes a vicious circle. Further more the owner then loses confidence with the dog and begins to anticipate other dogs appearing by keeping the dog on a tight lead, becoming tense and on the look out. This behaviour can alert the dog to anticipate another dog approaching and both owner and dog become agitated during the whole of the walk.

So what can we do about it?

Firstly it is very important that we try and understand why our dog is reacting in this way before trying to rectify the problem. Using a blanket approach of becoming "top dog" yourself is not very helpful if your dog is frightened to death of other dogs because it was badly savaged as a young puppy. More often than not, there could be several underlying reasons why your dog is behaving in this way and it is advisable to seek professional help at this stage. A good recommended companion animal behaviourist will help you to understand these reasons and prepare a behavioural modification programme to help you. They will also offer you support during this process. To help you there is a list of professional organisations at the back of this book.

The following two case histories show how complex this problem can be.

Sophie's story:

The first case involves Sophie a Collie Cross who frantically lunged against the lead choking and squealing every time she saw any other dog. Her owner became extremely embarrassed and tried to stop her from doing this by pulling her back, telling her off and pushing her bottom onto the ground. It didn't work and Sophie squealed increasingly louder and louder every time she met another dog. Was it anything to do with lack of socialisation? I here you ask. Well no, Sophie was born in a kitchen surrounded by other family dogs and children, played with and allowed regular access to the garden. Her new owners were experienced dog owners and knew the importance of early learning and enrolled her in puppy training classes at four months of age where interestingly this behaviour started. It turned out Sophie was very good at obedience and agility and loved these classes especially the period where all dogs were allowed to run about in a free for all. During this time she chased all the other dogs in sight. She seemed to enjoy these classes so much that her new owners took her several times a week. However, Sophie's behaviour changed direction and she soon began to focus more on chasing other dogs than the actual classes themselves. Once she had caught the dog she would make a yipping noise and worried at its legs until it ran away again or turned on her, in which case she would try another dog. This chasing behaviour became so frequent that the dog trainer finally asked the owners to take Sophie home and not to bring her back. Even though she knew all the commands, Sophie was simply not listening anymore and was becoming disruptive. She had so much fun fulfilling her need to chase (she was part Collie after all) that she became quite distressed when all the fun suddenly stopped. Her owners tried to compensate with a ball, but she showed no interest in that, or a Frisbee, rope, squeaky banana or food treats. All she wanted was to chase other dogs.

Sophie was not playing at being the "top dog" or protecting her owner or wanting to fight. She was simply a Collie, programmed to chase and had learned that chasing dogs was the most fun of all. The more rewards she got from chasing dogs the more dogs she chased. Therefore, we had to teach her that charging after other dogs was not much fun and that chasing something else was much better. The owners also had to change the way they dealt with Sophie's response towards other dogs by not reacting and reinforcing the behaviour but by remaining calm and telling her by using their own bored body language that there was nothing to get excited at.

Dogs are not too good at understanding long complicated sentences but they are good at reading body language.

The owners are not helping their dog or themselves if they become anxious. Sophie is still going to react badly in the early stages of the programme however they react so what's the point of causing unnecessary stress. In this case the owners were to react as blandly as they could and smile cheerily at the other dog owners. It is common sense that if you look worried about your dog's behaviour other people are going to also. On the other hand if you act like you're not bothered by how your dog is behaving and that it is quite normal for dogs to squeal like pigs and froth at the mouth, then the other owner, although looking puzzled, will be much less worried about the situation. And you can always pop on dark glasses and a floppy hat.

Initially Sophie had to be walked away from other dogs as the stimulus to chase was too powerful for her and was given something more appropriate to chase. These came in the form of two footballs in nets and linked together. When you pushed one football the momentum of it pulled the other past it. Sophie enjoyed playing with these in the back garden but still showed no sign of being interested whilst out walking. She had begun to associate going out for walks with other dogs appearing and would constantly be on the look out. Therefore, we had to teach her that going out for walks did not guarantee she would meet other dogs. Poor old Sophie spent the next few months going for the oddest walks, lots of boring short ones and long ones in dog-less places. However, she started to take more notice of a ball and her favourite game was finding the treat in a tree. It was important at this stage that Sophie was not further frustrated by the lack of fun in her life and that she gained lots of appropriate attention. It was also advised that Sophie tried Flyball a game where the dog weaves in and out of posts towards a machine that *shoots out a tennis ball and the dog catches it and races back to its owner. It is usually run as a team event and is a great focus for Collies that are highly motivated to work. The owners contacted a very good club and began to teach her, initially with no other dogs present, how to play. Sophie loved it and so did the owners and gradually they introduced Sophie to other more focused dogs that ignored Sophie's attempts to make them run and soon she was having the time of her life chasing tennis balls instead. Eventually Sophie stopped reacting in such an excited manner and the squealing ceased. However, it took six months before Sophie could be walked off lead again and even now if she sees a dog running she will sometimes chase it.*

Sophie was born to chase and nothing the owners could do would ever stop her needing to perform that. We did not try to make her stop squealing and pulling by punishing her or acting like a "top dog", but instead re-directed her focus towards something else more appropriate instead. There was no quick fix, no waving of a behavioural wand and it was a slow process but in the end we have a happy owner and a happy dog, job done.

Hectors story:

The second case involved Hector a beautiful Airedale who barked and lunged towards other dogs and often managed to pull his female owner over. Funnily enough he never did it when being walked by his male owner or when off the lead in his presence. Now Airedales are the greatest breed of dog on this planet, probably in the whole universe. I've got one and am not biased in any way! However, they can act in quite a stubborn way at times and many, when asked to do something, take around 5 seconds to do it. You have to earn compliance with an Airedale. Most Airedales will never make Crufts obedience champions simply because they don't particularly see the need to jump through hoops or bother much deciding on which handkerchief to pick up. Airedales are much happier bouncing around like Tiggers and sniffing under bushes.

Natural ability

Not all dogs make great agility, hunting, retrieving or obedience champions just like we can't all win Nobel Peace prizes or run the 100 meters in under four minutes.
It's important to remember this.

The times an owner has told me how disappointed they are that their dog is doing badly in training classes due to its lack of retrieving. "Oh he chases them all right but doesn't always bring them back" one owner bemoaned disappointedly. The dog in question happened to be a Jack Russell, a breed that we humans have designed to chase and kill rodents with great tenacity. A Jack Russell is not a retriever. You wouldn't want live rats handed to you at regular intervals now would you? Dogs like humans have different abilities and do not always fit into our perception of the perfect model.

So why was Hector acting aggressively towards other dogs only when he was out with his female but not his male owner?

Whilst having a nice cup of tea and a biscuit (things we behaviourists like doing best) and listening to the owners describe Hector I learned that he followed his female owner everywhere she went in the house and garden. He would also try and sit between the two owners if they cuddled up together, constantly nudged and brought her an endless supply of socks. His female owner responded to his every move by stroking, patting, talking to him and retrieving socks.

His aggressive behaviour towards other dogs started when he reached 20 months and became increasingly worse over the following year. At first it was only directed towards large dogs (possibly male, the owners were not sure about this). However, more recently he had begun to respond to every size of dog and his female owner had stopped taking him out alone. So why was Hector only showing this behaviour with her?

The clues lay with the female owner's reaction to Hectors advances. She responded to them all which is a very human thing to do. Thus Hector had begun to regard her as a very important resource and may have been unwilling to see her run off with the dog across the road especially if it was another large male dog. In other words he had started to show competitive aggression towards other dogs since he was now maturing into an adult dog with certain needs. The owners had him castrated but it didn't seem to make any difference to his competitive behaviour.

During the consultation I accompanied the female owner and Hector on a walk and observed his and her reaction. Every time a dog approached Hector became very stiff with his tail and ears erect. When the other dog got closer Hector then began to bark, show his teeth and lunge towards the dog. The owner's response, even before Hector reacted, was to pull on the lead and she became understandably very anxious.

An interesting and very significant incidence occurred during this walk. It was getting dark and the owner saw what she thought was a man with a dog. Immediately Hector started to react and began to lunge even though in reality there wasn't any one there. The female owner just thought there was and Hector had responded to her triggers. He had learned to associate his owner's reactions to approaching dogs and could predict their appearance.

We took several approaches to help rectify this problem;

i. *To help reduce Hectors competitive behaviour towards his female owner she was advised not to respond to any of Hectors attention seeking nudges, sock bringing, staring and whining. During the consultation Hector tried many different behaviours to gain her attention. He stared hard at her and began to bark, he brought her a shoe, a chewed up teddy and finally a cushion. He continually asked to be let out but when the door was opened for him, in case he wanted to go to the loo, he just sat there. He tried to nudge the male owners hand and then mine. He sat right in between all of us trying to catch eye contact and then tried to jump up onto the sofa. We ignored all these behaviours.*

ii. *Once Hector had settled both the owners rewarded him for showing calm behaviour using a treat. However, it is very important to remember that a dog is a social creature and needs company and interaction. Therefore, the owners were shown how to play the learn to earn game (described previously) and were told to play this often using different rewards in different environments. The owners could give him as much attention as they liked, as long as they initiated it first and as long as Hector was called over to them and asked to wait (defer) before receiving it. The game was also used when Hector got up to follow his female owner to the loo. The male owner would call him over in a jolly voice and play the game. Hector soon learned that better things were on offer than constantly having to follow his owner around. He thus associated his female owner leaving with nice things happening to him rather than bad. Once this issue was addressed Hector became a lot more relaxed around the house as he didn't have to keep getting up all the time.*

iii.   *Secondly we had to address the behaviour of the owner whilst out walking and the triggers she was inadvertently giving out. Her husband didn't react in the same way and kept Hector on a relatively loose lead. Therefore, she had to work on relaxing and allowing Hector more rope. This sounds easy but it is actually a very hard thing to achieve since the female owner had lost confidence and felt a great deal of anxiety when out walking with him. Confidence is often difficult to regain. Therefore, initially she only walked him for short walks, more often and in areas where there were relatively few dogs. Of course it's easy for me to say walk your dog where there are no other dogs as in many areas this can be almost impossible. But if one does pop out from behind a bush it is important to remain calm.*

iv.   *Then when Hectors owner spotted a dog instead of reacting by pulling him back she was to relax, take a deep breath and play the game with him using a treat reward, but only if Hector had spotted but not reacted to the dog. This meant getting the distance between them and other dog right. Too far and Hector would not have been aware of it and too close Hector would have started to react. Not impossible but hard work and a lot of commitment.*

Is giving a reward bribery?

Some owners will feel that giving a dog a treat in the midst of problem behaviour is simply a bribe. However, a bribe is very different to rewarding the dog for behaving well. If, for instance, the dog was barking madly towards another dog and the owner frantically waved a treat in front of it, then this is a bribe. The owner would be rewarding the dog for barking. The dog would then carry on barking. If on the other hand the dog had spotted another dog but it was not quite close enough to stimulate a reaction, the owner may able to distract the dog by producing a treat or a toy. They could then ask it to sit and wait calmly and thus the dog would be rewarded for this behaviour and not for barking.

This is an important and fundamental difference between rewarding for good behaviour and bribery.

After a few weeks Hector's behaviour had started to improve and now when he spots another dog he sits and waits calmly for a treat. However, Hector is not "cured"! If his owners did not follow the programme consistently Hectors aggressive behaviour towards other dogs may easily reoccur. He has not magically become the "perfect" dog. However, what they have achieved is better management of the situation. They have achieved their goal. They have also have taught Hector that he does not have to compete for his female owner any more and that others dogs are actually fun things to have around.

These are just two examples of dogs showing aggression towards other dogs. I hope they show how individual each case is and how important it is to look at the bigger picture of what's going on and why. I have seen hundreds of other case's all as different and all needing a slightly different approach to help address the problem and no doubt I shall see a few more.

I would just add like to add that dog-dog aggression is less likely to occur if puppies are allowed to interact with other dogs when they are young so they can learn for themselves what is and what isn't sociably acceptable within the doggy world.

Food treats?

Some owners may not like the idea of using food treats and if your dog is highly motivated by toys then use these. However, most dogs are motivated by food. There is nothing wrong with giving a treat at appropriate times but do be aware of weight gain problems. Use a high quality treat (meat strips, cheese, sausage) to begin with and then reduce the number of times, the amount and quality (mixer, chicken, low fat treats) as your dog progresses. You may have to adjust the amount you are feeding your dog or make sure that it receives more exercise. If you use a jolly voice whilst your dog is eating the treat, this will then condition your dog to react to your voice and after a while, your jolly voice will do just as well.

The use of reward based training methods is far superior than the use of punishment based ones, especially if your dog is overly bold or nervous in character.

Chapter Five

Problems with destructive behaviour when left "Home Alone".

Another common problem dealt with by behaviourists is that of leaving a dog home alone. For some owners their dog has to be taken everywhere they go since if it stayed at home the sofa would disappear. Others return to pulled-up carpets, chewed door frames and some to puddles or worse all over the kitchen floor. I have known large dogs to squeeze through cat flaps, dig holes through brick walls and in particular a Staffordshire Terrier that jumped clean through a closed glass window. To be unable to leave your dog home alone causes considerable anxiety to both dog and owner and enormous inconvenience especially if the dog will not even tolerate being left in a car.

So why does this happen?

- Is it due to the dog not being socialised sufficiently when young?
- Is it acting as "Top dog" and demanding your return?
- Does it want a friend to play with?
- Is it just being naughty?

Destructive behaviour and anxiety when left could occur for many reasons but not generally for any of the above.

So why are some dogs so destructive when left?

Dogs are sociable creatures and naturally live in groups which work together to secure territories in which there are important resources such as food, shelter and water. Intruder dogs are chased away and there are plenty of dogs to warn others against predators. Dogs, therefore, are likely to feel safe within their group and will probably not feel so secure when left on their own. It is not natural for a dog to be "home alone" and it is no wonder that some domestic dogs show anxiety behaviours when left. However, most dogs seem to cope relatively well when left so what makes these ones different to the others that can't.

The answer lies in the fact that all dogs are different:
- They have all had different upbringings
- They have all had different experiences
- They all have different genetic characters.
- They all have different owners.

Just as some humans are more insecure than others so are dogs.

There are many reasons why a dog may show some anxiety when left:
- In some cases the dog may have had a bad experience whilst being in the home such as a loud thunder storm or next doors having their new conservatory fitted. In this case they may associate being left in the home with scary things happening to them.
- Others have a greater need to be with their other group members (their owners) and become anxious when left.
- There are dogs that simply get bored more easily than others.

➢ Some even enjoy stealing crisp packets from the bin and have learned that they can do this when their owners are absent.

➢ Sometimes it's the anticipation of the owners returning that triggers this behaviour especially if the owners are angry. The dog may not necessarily understand that they are angry purely because of the mess they find.

Big Brother

The best way of trying to get to the bottom of why a dog is behaving in this way is to set up a video camera (keep it away from the dogs reach). This can be actually quite difficult for the owners to watch as the dog is sometimes clearly distressed. If the dog reacts straight away to being left and continues in this vein for most of the time it can be surmised that it has anxiety problems. The behaviours to look out for are continual pacing around, whining, barking, panting, yawning, licking lips, jumping up at doors, persistent chewing either furniture or itself, and inappropriate toileting. You may find the dog seems quite happy at first and then suddenly becomes distressed. This may be due to an outside noise, a postman, neighbours leaving for work etc. If, however, the dog seems quite happy and relaxed, goes to sleep and then after an hour or two begins to mooch about looking for things to do then it is probably bored. In this case it is important that the owners consider the amount of time the dog is left and to give it something to do.

Simply giving a dog something to do if it is showing true anxiety problems probably won't help much and nor will acting like you are the "Top dog". Instead seek professional help.

Use of Crates heaven or hell?

Many owners with destructive dogs resort to leaving them in a crate (an indoor kennel usually made of wire). Personally I like these but only if the dog does. If you have to force the dog into it when you leave then it's defeating the object somewhat, which is to teach your dog that being left is not a bad experience. If on the other hand you can teach your dog that the crate is the best thing since sliced sausage then it may help in allowing your dog to feel more secure when left. You can do this by introducing it slowly to your dog and filling it full of nice things and its own smelly blanket. I prefer to pop a blanket over the top to create a more den like effect.

Initially leave the door of the crate open so it can come and go and allow it to sleep there quietly when it feels the need. Once it has become used to it, begin to sometimes shut the door but only when you are in the house. Then you can begin to shut it and pop out of the back door for a few seconds. Slowly build this up over the weeks until you can leave the door shut for a few minutes. If at any time the dog becomes distressed, stay close to the crate and wait until it has calmed down. Then open the door but do not acknowledge the dog if it comes over to you in an excited manner. You do not want to teach your dog that escaping the crate is rewarding. Start the process again but go back to a stage where the dog is calm. Introducing a crate at the puppy stage is advisable and hopefully the puppy will find the crate a safe and secure place in which to be left.

Never us a crate as a punishment area.

What not to do!

Some owners are advised to reprimand the dog once they have returned by showing them the damage and telling the dog off. Showing dogs how to do things does not work. All the dog will learn is that they will be punished every time the owner returns. This is likely to make the dog even more anxious when left. They will have no concept that digging up the shag pile is the behaviour that makes their owner angry. After all the dog has performed many behaviours whilst the owner is away. Some owners make the remark that their dog **must** know their behaviour was bad since every time they return the dog looks guilty. Yes it probably does look guilty but what the dog is really trying to communicate is that it doesn't want to be punished. The dog is trying to appease and yet the owner is still angry. This can be very confusing for a dog that will, after all, have no idea why the owner is cross. All the dog did was to try and escape and to dig its way to freedom to get to the rest of its group. "Ah" but I hear you cry, "My dog only looks guilty after it has messed on the kitchen floor". So the dog has learned that you are cross and it has something to do with pooh. It will still have no idea that you want it to stop poohing when you leave it and that poohing is wrong, how could it possibly understand such a difficult concept. You wouldn't expect your 18month old child to understand this so why should your dog?

What to do instead?

Remain calm and ignore the mess until you can clean it up out of view of the dog. This can be a hard feat to achieve so a good bottle of Sauvignon Blanc chilling away in the fridge is an essential tool. Then pick up your phone and ask for help.

Pheromones

There are pheromone diffusers (DAP) currently on the market that may be used in conjunction with the crate that profess to help a dog feel more relaxed. The pheromones that are released are similar to the ones given off by a mother dog with puppies to help them feel secure. They can be placed close to the crate to help create a secure ambiance.

However, if nothing much changes or the problem is very severe seek help from a professional companion animal behaviourist.

To help explain the many different reasons why dogs may become destructive when left I am going to discuss two very different case histories.

Max's story:

The worse case of destructive behaviour I have seen to date involved a young farm Collie called Max whose owner had fallen foul of the promise that farm Collies make incredibly good pets. Max and his owner lived in a small terraced house in the middle of a large industrial city. His owner worked full time but did pop back at dinner times to take him out.

When I walked into this small terraced house I simply couldn't believe my eyes. The sitting room and kitchen areas downstairs were completely demolished. There was not a stick of furniture to be found or a door frame or a skirting board or any electrical sockets. There was a hole where the fireplace used to be and a badly chewed cast iron radiator. The windows were smeared with slobber and he had nearly finished chewing through the frames. The small back yard was inches deep in faeces and not much else. The owner had managed to keep Max from going up stairs by putting up a stair gate with extra chicken wire. The owner was at her wits end as she had really tried to keep on top of things.

Max wasn't a "bad" dog. He wasn't aggressive towards humans or other dogs, he went to the toilet outside and he wasn't particularly attention seeking. However, inside the house he was about the most anxious dog I have ever seen. He spent all his time pacing up and down, panting and salivating. However, once outside and walking he relaxed and thoroughly enjoyed the experience. The owner walked him as often as she could and spent 1-2 hours a day doing so. But Max just wasn't the sort of dog you could keep locked up. He was designed by years of breeding to work a 12 hour shift.

In this case Max was re-homed to an experienced Collie owner with a lot of land. With the best will in the world a few extra toys and a pheromone diffuser wasn't going to touch this dog. His was a happy ending but many do not end like this.

The take home message is this case highlights the importance of researching breed type and having the available time and space to be able to give a dog what it needs.

Jazz's story

Max's case was an extreme one, a more usual case concerned the behaviour of a lovely Labrador cross called Jazz. She was a rescue dog and her new owners gave her a lovely new home when she 14 months old. They had little history regarding her previous life as she was found wandering around the city streets feeding from dustbins. She was very thin and covered in fleas and had since developed a bad skin reaction to them. Jazz did not know how to walk on a lead or any of the basic training instructions.

When her new owners fell in love with her and bought her into their home she settled in very quickly and remarkably they had no trouble with toilet training. The only major problem they had was that they could not leave the house without Jazz crying loudly for the whole duration of their absence and trying to dig her way out through the wooden door frame. Luckily for them, as this is not always the case, they had understanding neighbours who did not call out the local council environment agency. But sensibly the owners tried to rectify the problem by calling their local vet who referred them on to me and a visit was arranged the following week.

What a behaviourist should be asking you

In all behavioural cases taking detailed notes of the dog's character, history and its day to day routine is crucial in gaining a better insight to the problem. Watching how the dog behaves with its owners and visitors is also important and equally vital is how the owners react to the dog. A quick 10 minute chat over the phone rarely suffices and a professional behaviourist will never give advice based on this approach. It is normal for the behaviourist to spend many hours with their clients watching and learning. A behavioural modification programme and report will be worked out for you and a copy will be sent to your referring vet. A good behaviourist will also offer support over the weeks and months during behavioural modification and will work alongside your vet if drug therapy is necessary. To be sure you are receiving the best advice seek a qualified and recommended companion animal behaviourist. The Association of Pet Behaviour Counsellors (APBC) promotes and develops the profession of pet behaviour counselling and provides a network of specialist counsellors throughout the UK. All full members have to have the highest professional standards, knowledge and expertise and a rigorous selection procedure is in place to assess all applicants. A list of APBC members in your area can be found on their website www.apbc.org.uk. There is also a list of fully accredited certified clinical animal behaviourists on the ASAB website www.asab.nottingham.ac.uk.

On entering the house Jazz came bounding over full of enthusiasm but soon settled down and we all had a nice cup of tea and a biscuit. Before my visit I suggested the owners set up a video camera and tape her behaviour.

Jazz was left for 30 minutes and immediately after her owners closed the door, she began to pace up and down, scratched at the carpet, jumped all over the furniture and howled . At no point did she relax or lay in her basket or played with her toys even though some were filled with tasty treats. When the owners came back in although they didn't reprimand Jazz for pulling up the carpet they did sigh and shake their heads.

The whole process was heartbreaking to watch and the owners felt very distressed. The owners were quite clear that they never reprimanded Jazz for making the mess since they had read a book which had advised them not to do this. The reason given for this behaviour was that the dog was behaving in this way because dogs viewed their owners as puppies and became worried about them when they left. They followed the advice given in the book and began to act as "Top Dog" and began to ignore her. However, this had an odd effect on Jazz and she became a lot quieter and not her usual self. The owners described her as "depressed" so they stopped doing it. Jazz brightened up but still couldn't cope with being left.

The dangers of behaving as "Top Dog".

Using a blanket approach of curing all ills by becoming "top dog" can cause frustration in dogs that expect and enjoy a fuss, toys, treats or their dinner at certain times. Taking this away in an attempt to behave like a "top dog" is very punishing to some dogs especially if they lack confidence or are nervous to begin with. What you are effectively doing is punishing them for something that they will not understand. On the other hand this approach may also be seen as very challenging to pushy confident dogs and may cause an increase in aggressive behaviour towards the owner since the dog is more likely to up the stakes to get what it wants. I can not state enough times how important it is to find a qualified and professional behaviourist who can help diagnose the problem successfully and design a behavioural modification programme to fit each individual dog.

So to help Jazz we began to teach her that being left was actually ok. The reason behind her distress probably stemmed from the fact she felt more secure when group members were present. She may have associated being on her own with bad things happening to her whilst roaming the streets or even distressed by being in the rescue kennels.

Kennel Stress

Being locked away in a small concrete block surrounded by other distressed dogs can be a harrowing experience especially when as a dog you do not understand the concept of what a lock is. For all you know another of these distressed dogs may appear and attack you at any minute. With the best will in the world locking dogs away in kennels can cause them to become stressed and it is important to re-home them as soon as possible. However, for some dogs this can be enormously difficult since their behaviour behind bars puts potential owners off. Much time and effort goes into helping these cases cope better with life behind bars and my heart goes out to those well meaning, often underpaid and hard working individuals involved with this process.

Therefore, it was important that Jazz began to learn that being left was not a bad experience but a good one. To do this we looked at several areas:

1) Find out what triggers alert your dog to you leaving

Dogs are good at leaning triggers that alert them to you leaving, as are small children. All I have to do is put my earrings in and my 5 year old daughter will immediately demand to know where I am going? Most mums and dog owners at this stage feel incredibly guilty and try to explain why they have to go and how quickly they will be back. Dogs have little concept of time. Saying "I'll only be a few minutes, now don't pull up the carpet and if you are good you will get a treat" means to many dogs" you will now feel bad very bad indeed". Dogs contrary to belief do not have a strong command of the English language although some can certainly recognise lots of words like, walk, bye, sit, dinner,

Auntie Betty, hello, fetch, come here, etc they have great difficulty making sense of long complicated sentences. Therefore, it was important that Jazz's owners recognised these triggers and stopped performing them. In Jazz's case the triggers were:

> ➢ *The owners picking up their house keys, therefore, they had to begin to pick them up and sit back down again. This allowed Jazz to learn that picking up keys did not always mean her owners were leaving.*

> ➢ *Another was putting on outdoor shoes, so the owners began to walk to their car in their slippers whilst holding their shoes or putting their shoes into the car the night before.*

> ➢ *Saying "good bye see you later" and "be good". Therefore, the owners stopped saying this.*

2) De-sensitise your dog into being left

The owners then had to pop out of the door and immediately straight back in again as if was the most natural thing in the world. They had to do this so often over the next few days that Jazz got bored with it, so bored in fact that she didn't bother to react at all. Once she was happy and relaxed at them doing this they popped out, waited for two seconds and popped in again. When they came back they did not make a big deal of it and simply carried on with normal life. Once Jazz was happy and ignored them they would give her a cue that she could come and greet them. This was a simple verbal command and If I remember correctly this was "What ho".

The next stage was leaving her for five seconds and once she was happy with this period of time they gradually over weeks increased the time she was left.

3) Create a secure place for your dog to hide in

Whilst they were doing this they were also advised to design a hidey-hole area for Jazz to retreat to. Somewhere she could feel and safe and secure in. They could have used an indoor crate but they used a cupboard beneath the stairs instead, in which they placed used blankets, some toys, treats and an unwashed somewhat whiffy tee shirt belonging to the male owner. Dogs have an acute sense of smell and can find security in surrounding themselves with familiar smells, not unlike a security blanket that many children hang on to and woe betide Mummy if she ever tries to wash it. Jazz was encouraged to sleep in this area whilst the owners were in the house especially when the vacuum cleaner appeared. The owners also left a radio playing on a station they would normally be listening to. Jazz was also given some reward based training exercises to learn and the owners were advised to make sure she received at least two good quality walks a day.

Quality walks

A quality walk is where the dog gets to use its brain as well as just given physical exercise. The dog will receive some basic training exercises and the owner might play hide the treat, throw the ball or ask the dog to jump over logs or weave around trees. The dog will be allowed to have a good sniff about so it can read and send its pee-mails, follow a scent, meet other dogs and run very fast. In other words the dog gets to enjoy the walk and is not just paraded around the block stuck to its owner's leg.

Now this sounds like a very easy programme to put in place, but it actually takes a lot of commitment and means that the owners could not leave the dog for longer than the time period they had reached. These poor people spent five weeks working on Jazz and they reached the point where she was happy to be left for an hour or two. They still noticed, however, that if there was heavy rain or thunder Jazz would still sometimes pull the carpet up but over time she began to cope better with being left.

Shall I get another dog to help my dog cope better?

Sometimes getting another dog provides immediate peace and quiet and sometimes you end up getting two problem dogs for the price of one. It may be a wise move to borrow a friendly dog that doesn't mind being left and set up the video camera. What is important is understanding why your dog behaves this way and seek advice.

Chapter Six

Pulling on the lead.

As a behaviourist I am sometimes called on to help cope with training problems and amongst the most common ones encountered is that of consistent pulling and tugging on the lead. For some dogs it doesn't matter which new expensive halter design they are fitted with, pulling to go forwards, even if it becomes uncomfortable, is still preferable to standing still. I have come across dogs that have rubbed their necks raw with pulling and owners that have ended up with repetitive strain injuries.

So why pull when it hurts so much to do so?

Well first we can look at what walking might mean to a dog. In the wild domestic/feral dogs spend their days, amongst other activities, protecting their territory, sleeping, hunting and scavenging for food. To find food they have to spend some time looking for it since it is unlikely that someone will pop out from behind a bush and offer them a big bowl full of meaty chunks. It takes time and energy to hunt for it and thus dogs tend to become highly motivated and excited at the prospect. Since our domestic dogs are also likely to have this allotted time to hunt wired into their natural daily activity pattern, going for a walk has taken the place of going hunting and it is very normal for a dog to become excited.

When out walking a dog can read and send its pee-mails, meet other dogs and people, run about and chase things. Therefore most dogs find walking highly rewarding. It is, therefore, understandable that some dogs may want to go forwards quickly and if they learn that pulling on the lead enables them to do this they will carry on pulling even if they are feeling uncomfortable or in pain since the benefits of going forwards out way the costs of getting hurt.

What pulling on the lead probably does not mean

- Pulling on the lead does not necessarily mean that they see themselves as the "top dog" as top dogs always go first.
- That they have never been on a lead before.
- That they walk faster than you do.

Pulling on the lead so hard that it damages both dog and owner is not desirable but this doesn't mean that you can't allow your dog a little loose rein.

Personally unless the dog is being trained to work in the ring I feel it unfair for a dog to be constantly kept on a tight lead when out walking at all times. A dog needs to sniff, pee and have a healthy interest in the outside world. It must be very boring for the "perfect" dog being stuck to its owner's leg and having to ignore all those alluring messages posted on lampposts and bushes.

What we can do about pulling?

We can teach our dog that pulling on the lead gets them nowhere and that being on a loose lead does! To illustrate this I have chosen to use another case history.

Gus's story.

Gus was six months at the time and a very strong male Staffordshire Bull Terrier. As soon as the owners even thought about taking him for a walk he would begin to spin around squeaking and squealing madly. Once the lead was produced he spun even more quickly and would try and bite at it. It took his owners some time to actually put the lead on and Gus would try and grab at the owners hand in which the lead was in. Once the door was open he charged towards it knocking everyone and everything out of his way and hurled himself towards the front gate of the garden. After attacking the gate ferociously to get it open he pulled and pulled his owners along the road jumping and grabbing at their hands. He even urinated as he was doing it and could easily soak his owner's trouser legs within a 100 yard distance.

They tried everything from trussing him up into what can only be described as a straight jacket to physically pushing him to the ground. They tried bribery, shouting, shaking tins full of pebbles and ignoring him but nothing worked. Gus became so excited at the prospect of a walk he became uncontrollable.

I purposely visited the owners and Gus during the time he normally went out for a walk and quietly watched his behaviour as the clock ticked towards the dreaded walkie time. Around 10 minutes to go, Gus started to whine and became more alert. He started to pace around the room, looking towards his owners who responded with words like "not yet Gus in a minute" and "hang on". This excited Gus even more. They then started to get a little anxious and kept trying to tell Gus that it wasn't time yet. Gus just wound up and up until he was beginning to spin and squeal. Finally the owners said "Ok Gus come on then walkie time".

The sudden explosion from Gus after hearing the word "Walkie" was incredible and he set off screaming, squealing, spinning and urinating. The lead came out and after a few minutes of trying to put it on with no success they decided to slip a rope lead on instead over his head which led to Gus choking himself and turning quite blue at times. And off we went with Gus pulling, squealing and turning blue along the road. The owners confessed that they very rarely took him out anymore on the road but instead took him by car to a nearby beach where he would jump out, throw himself about for a bit and then trot quite nicely by their side for the rest of the walk. I could quite see why they did this but Gus would need to be on the lead at some point so it was important that he learned to calm down.

On the homeward turn Gus calmed down enough to start some work with him. It was obvious that no device was going to help him as his owners had tried everything going, so Gus had to learn to help himself.

As Gus pulled I asked the owners to calmly resume the skiing position (lead in both hands with knees bent) and wait calmly. Gus did not like this and squealed and pulled and pulled and squealed. Five minutes later he sat down and the lead went slack, at this point I asked the owners to take a step forwards, Gus charged away again so the owners stood still again and only moved forward when Gus stopped pulling and the lead went slack. As you can guess it took us a very long time to get home. However, it didn't take Gus very long to learn that sitting down allowed him to go forwards since when he sat the lead went slack and he could lunge forwards again. It was a slow process and we received a few funny looks but we did all get home eventually with relatively ache free arms.

Why did Gus pull so much?

Gus was a naturally excitable dog as many Staffies are and enjoyed walks so much he went over the top when his internal body clock told him that one was imminent. His owners also reinforced this by talking to him and triggering his behaviour. Even though they told him they were not ready, all Gus understood was that those particular words said in that tone meant walkies were imminent. The lead appearing sent Gus into a frenzy of chemical reactions resulting in spinning, squealing and urinating behaviour. Therefore, it was important that Gus began to learn that walks could be boring things instead and not just the exciting sometimes frustrating and painful experiences he had previously associated them with.

How to calm him down?

The owners were asked:

- *Not to trigger any reaction from Gus by speaking to him if he whined and not to produce the lead at that point.*
- *To remain calm before walks.*
- *To change the walk times so they were not so routinely set.*
- *To train Gus that before he got any sort of reward his bottom had to be placed firmly on the ground using the learn to earn game (described previously)*
- *They then had to teach him to sit before the lead went on. If he bounced up and tried to grab the lead it was taken away above the owners head with a firm "no".*
- *They also had to put the lead on and take it off again on a regular basis to teach Gus that an appearing lead did not always mean he was going for a walk.*
- *Since Gus was so over excited when going through the door he was taught to sit and wait by the door by opening it a few inches and shutting it again if he tried to charge through.*

- *Once Gus had calmed down he was taken initially via the car a short distance away from the house and walked back, stopping if the lead became tight and starting when it was loose. This allowed Gus to learn that not all walks were exciting.*
- *Once Gus had begin to settle down the trips were extended over the following weeks until he was calmly walking back to the house and not pulling.*
- *Gus was then allowed to walk out through the front door. If he pulled and squealed he was calmly walked back in again.*

Gus will always be a little excited about going for walks and that is quite acceptable but he no longer squeals or grabs at hands and has learned that walking is actually a pleasant experience. The owners spent a great of deal time working with Gus and were remarkably patient. It took them some considerable time to achieve their aims but it was worth it in the end. They now have a much calmer Gus, their arms are firmly back in their sockets and their trouser legs are dry, Job done!

It is quite acceptable to allow your dog to walk on a loose lead and allow him some access to the lampposts and bushes of this world. It is also a good idea for your dog to walk between you and the road side.

It is not acceptable to have your dog pulling your arms out of their sockets or charging across roads. But If you stop (do not pull back) every time your dogs lead tightens and only move forward when it is loose your dog will quickly learn how to walk calmly and you can both enjoy the experience.

Chapter Seven

Dealing with constant attention seeking behaviour.

Why is it that some dogs seem to take go to great pains to steal a pair of your pants and run around the garden with them in their mouths? Why do some constantly bring you toys to play with or howl persistently when you are trying to talk to someone on the phone? The answer is probably because "They can". They have learned that if they steal your best Calvin Klein's, offer you squeaky or shout really loudly <u>you react</u>. You may not always react in a positive way but for some dogs any attention at all is good attention and it has always amazed me the lengths some dogs go to get it.

So why do some dogs need to have constant attention whilst others do not? Well again we can look at how domestic/feral dogs behave naturally. They live in social groups and work together to defend a territory and the resources it contains. Some dogs are genetically stronger physically and mentally and generally make the decisions regarding what, when and how they will hunt and who to chase away. These dogs gain rank by challenging other group members and gain certain privileges over them:

- They get to eat and drink first.
- Gain more mating opportunities.
- Claim the best den areas.

However, the hierarchy within a group is not set in stone and this is an important point to remember. It does not mean that these stronger dogs always gain the advantage and it depends very much on how much they need the resource. For instance a starving female dog with puppies may challenge a usually stronger individual for food because she is so hungry. The stronger dog may have just eaten and might decide not to risk injury so allows this other female to take the food. A gaggle of scientists hiding in a nearby bush may mistakenly assume that the female with puppies is the stronger dog. Therefore, making such conclusions by just observing single interactions can be misleading.

When dealing with attention seeking behaviour it is important that you have a clear understanding of why your dog is behaving in such a way. Your particular problem dog may not even be challenging you for your high ranking position, it may instead be acting on a specific need it has for a particular resource. For instance farm Collies often show a particular need for working and some spend all day bringing toys to their owners to throw. They are not necessarily trying to usurp their owners from a high position within the group; it's just what they need to do this based on their genetic instincts to herd.

Some dogs simply learn that if they bite you on your bottom you leave them alone and so are more likely to bite you on the bottom the next time they wish you removed.

Common attention seeking behaviours

Persistent toy bringing

Constant nudging with head

Taking, presenting and running away with toys

Some howling, whining, barking behaviour

Pinching articles that make you react

Scratching at door but not wanting to go out

Any behaviour a dog may show that is directed at gaining a reaction

---

The over use of the "Top Dog" perspective can have grave problems if your dog is not seeking attention purely to get to the top. It may seem to the dog that it is being punished and it won't necessarily understand why. To illustrate this more clearly I will use two case histories that show how problem attention seeking behaviour can be presented by dogs to gain very different results.

Beau's story:

Beau was a lovely female Springer Spaniel who constantly barked at her owners, pulled at their trouser legs and brought them toys to play with night and day. She hardly slept and was barking to wake them up earlier and earlier each morning. She had been like this since the day they bought her home from a breeder who bred Spaniels as working dogs. The breeder had informed the owners that Beau would make a better pet than a working dog because she was very confident and bold. However, although Beau showed confidence towards humans she showed some very nervous behaviour towards noises such as thunder and fireworks and would spend her time during storms behind the sofa shaking. She also showed very submissive behaviour towards other dogs and would instantly roll on her back whenever she was approached.

The owners had previously asked advice from their local trainer/behaviourist who diagnosed Beau as showing "dominant" "Top Dog" behaviour and should be bought down a peg or two. The owners were told to ignore Beau for a lot of the time, make her wait downstairs before calling her up, always to walk in front of her and to take away her toys and only bring them out when it was play time. She was also carted off into a different room if she pulled at legs or barked. This regime did the trick; Beau stopped barking, stopped pulling their trouser legs and stopped bringing them toys. She also stopped wagging her tail, stopped approaching them and stopped behind the sofa. The owners were mortified and felt they had made her miserable so began to treat her as they had before. In a matter of days they were all back to square one. The owners then did what they should have done in the first place and asked their veterinary surgeon to check her over and refer her on to a qualified behaviourist.

Beau was not a "dominant" dog in the sense that she was trying to take over the world by behaving this way. This was clear when you looked at her behaviour towards other dogs and her reaction to loud noises (which also had to be dealt with). She was, however, an intelligent working dog who had been bred over generations to work for people and the work she was designed for was bringing her owner game. Since there weren't any pheasants lying around the house, Beau had substituted toys instead and was happily retrieving them for her owners. Since this behaviour was rewarding for her she quickly learned that if she kept it up, threw in a few barks and leg pulls she got to play these games more often.

Therefore, the owners did not have to worry, they were not being occupied by the SS (Springer Spaniel) division they just had a very high maintenance dog on their hands.

Advice given

i. The owners were asked to teach Beau how to come, sit and wait before getting any rewards and told they could play with her as often as they could as long as they initiated it.

ii. They were to ignore her advances, barking and leg pulling.

iii. Beau was allowed all sorts of fun toys to play with that offered her a way to puzzle out how to get at a small piece of dried dog food inside.

iv.	*The owners played hide the treat beneath plant pots in the garden and on walks behind trees. They jumped her over logs, wound around trees and played throw the rope toy, which looked a bit like a dead pheasant.*

They had to spend a lot of their time dealing with Beau's needs especially since she was still a young dog but at least they had a better behaved and happier one. Finally after a few weeks, during a wet Tuesday morning, Beau finally slept.

Tom's story

Now the second case history I would like to introduce you to is Tom a two year old Jack Russell Terrier cross. Tom had taken to standing in between his owners and barking at them. He constantly bought them toys but unlike Beau did not allow the owners to take the toys, instead he would present them and as soon as they bent down he growled and ran off across the room with the toy firmly clamped between his teeth. The crunch came when Tom started to urinate against visitor's legs and then proceed to jump up onto the sofa and mount their arms (especially arms with no sleeves). If the owners tried to confront Tom, he would bare his teeth and start snapping. The owners thought it was probably time to seek help. At this point Tom had not been castrated and arrangements were made to book him into surgery as soon as possible.

Is castration necessary?

Castration may help reduce the intensity and likelihood of problems related to sexual issues such as escape behaviour to reach a bitch in season, territorial marking or the humping of cushions. But it will not necessarily reduce aggression problems towards owners, other dogs, destructive behaviour when left or make your dog forget what it has already learned. Castration may be highly beneficial in certain cases, it stops unwanted pregnancies and may also prevent certain medical disorders; however, it is now believed that in some cases it may cause different problems. For instance, some dogs need that extra bit of help that the hormone testosterone gives them to cope with the challenges of other dogs. Take it away and the dog may become a little more fearful. The best advice is to seek the help of a fully qualified behaviourist to assess your dog and give advice on how you can help prevent any likely future problems that are individual to your dog. Allow your dog to mature and then decide between you whether or not castration will be of benefit.

As many Jack Russell owners are aware this breed does not always realise that they are "size challenged". They don't seem to notice that their legs are a third of the length of other dogs or that their teeth are tiny pearls in comparison to a Rottweiler's but are they bothered? They have the mental attitude of a pit bull, are tenacious and as tough as old boots. As was the case with Tom and even after the deed was done, he continued to urinate against peoples legs and mounted arms but now only if they were male and over 5 foot 8inchs. He still presented his owners with toys only to run away again and would still bark at his owners if they got too close to each other. Therefore, to compliment the recent operation the owners were asked to make sure Tom was under no illusion regarding his status and not to react to his consistent attention seeking behaviour.

> ➤ The owners were asked not to confront Tom by behaving aggressively themselves. This may have resulted in Tom reacting to the challenge and becoming more aggressive.

> ➤ All his attention seeking behaviour was to be ignored with the owners and visitors using their own body language to illustrate this. They took all eye contact away from him, turned their backs on him and walked away very theatrically.

> ➤ The owners taught him to show deference before they gave him any reward by playing the learn to earn game described previously.

> ➤ If a large man happened to enter the room, Tom was calmly placed onto a house line (collar and a length of thin rope) and the visitor was told to ignore him.

> ➤ When Tom showed calm behaviour he was immediately rewarded with more appropriate attention.

> ➤ If he made a lunge towards the arm, he was calmly reeled back in using the house line.

> ➤ When he presented his owners with toys they pretended they were not interested and began to look excitedly at another one. Once Tom no longer had hold of the "prize" toy he promptly dropped it and went to see what the owners were so interested in. Sometimes the owners ignored him and at other times they gave it to him but only after he had sat and waited first.

However, we mustn't forget that dogs have needs and since Jack Russell's were bred to kill rats Tom was given his very own rat to catch and kill in its very own drainpipe. The owners constructed a device where Tom could run through a very wide plastic drainpipe in which there was a toy rat on a rope that the owners could *pull. Tom loved this game and played catch the rat even when his owners were not present. Tom was given lots to do but in a more appropriate way and his status issues were addressed by using a non challenging method rather than a confrontational one. He still didn't like his owners having a cuddle much and was often asked to leave the bedroom on occasion but on the whole his behaviour improved dramatically. Tom will never be a "perfect" dog but his owners wouldn't want him any other way.*

The moral of this story is; be careful of assuming that your dog is showing "Dominant" "Top Dog" behaviour, as your subsequent treatment of it may cause more harm than good. If your dog does have status issues and if you are going to confront your dog on a one to one basis using physical techniques make sure that your dentures are firmly glued in first. Even better don't put yourself or your family at risk and apply techniques that are non-confrontational (see Chapter Two). As with any sort of aggressive behaviour it is wise to consult a qualified companion animal behaviourist who will asses your situation and design the right programme for you.

Chapter Eight

Aggression towards owners

One of the most harrowing problems I encounter as a companion animal behaviourist is when the much loved and cherished family pet turns on its owners. Dogs are often forgiven for showing aggressive behaviour towards strangers or other dogs as they are thought of as being protective but when it comes to showing aggression towards the owners and especially children life can become very stressful indeed.

So why does this happen?

There are many underlying reasons why this may happen.

- The dog may have some status issues and is telling you off.
- It may be that the dog has learned that acting in an aggressive way gains it a reward.
- The dog may be behaving in a competitive manner over resources that it finds particularly important.
- It may be in pain and is trying to tell you not to touch.
- It may be a female that has pups and is showing maternal aggression to protect them.
- It may have a serious medical problem that results in a change of behaviour
- It may be age related and the dog is starting to mature and becoming Kevin the teenager or it is much older and is turning into a Victor Meldrew.
- It may have had a poor early environment and has learned that becoming aggressive is the only way to get any food.

An increase in aggressive behaviour may be due to one or more of these reasons or a number of others and to help illustrate how complicated this problem can be let's meet Fred.

Fred's story

Fred was a three year old male West Highland White and had been acting like Victor Meldrew for the previous 18 months. The problems started when he was 15 months of age, around the time he would have been maturing into an adult. Fred did not like:

- *Being looked at.*
- *Being spoken to if he hadn't initiated it first.*
- *Being picked up.*
- *Being touched unless he asked to be.*
- *Anyone walking past him whilst he was asleep.*
- *Anyone coming anywhere near him whilst he was eating.*
- *His bottom being wiped.*
- *His feet being wiped.*
- *The brush.*
- *The bath.*

Thus Fred became somewhat smelly to have around.

Funnily enough and much to the embarrassment of his owners once Fred was manoeuvred gingerly into the car and coaxed carefully into the grooming parlour he became a pussy cat and was quite happy for his groomer to do absolutely what she liked to him.

However, if his owners were so bold to do any of the above Fred would bare his teeth and growl at them. If they did not comply and go away he would launch himself at their feet and bite them.

It was when he started to launch himself from the sofa in the general direction of crotch height that his owner's decided enough was enough. Now I have nothing against Westies! I used to work closely with "The Westie Rescue" Organisation in the UK, but up to now I have only ever been bitten by three dogs during my career and two of these were Westies. So imagine my delight at the thought of meeting Fred.

Over the phone Fred sounded a little like many of the problem Westies I had encountered but boy was I wrong. The moment I walked in and ignored him I knew it was going to take a lot of tea and biscuits to sort this little fellow out. Not only did Fred dislike his owners invading his space but he could hardly tolerate any other living being there either.

- He barked and chased away every bird that came into the garden.
- He barked at Butterflies.
- He barked at falling leaves.
- He rushed outside and barked at every aeroplane that flew over head and didn't stop until he Fred had successfully chased that away.
- And woe betides any cat that strayed into Fred's garden.
- He didn't bother much with hedgehogs though?

Unfortunately this meant that Fred spent most of his day pacing up and down grumbling and moaning and when he did manage to settle down he was soon up and growling as soon as anyone in the family dared to move.

All of the family had been bitten by him at some stage or another and luckily the children were all teenagers, but there was to be a young grandchild due soon and the owners were worried how Fred would cope with this. Personally I was more worried about the welfare of the family and the new baby but the family believed themselves to be at fault for some reason and blamed themselves.

So why was Fred behaving like a dictator?

i. *Was it that he was ungrateful?*

ii. *Did he see himself as the leader dog?*

iii. *Was he not properly socialised as a young puppy?*

iv. *Was it the fault of his breed's genetic makeup?*

Well probably not any of these things directly.

i. *I do not think that dogs have the cognitive ability to be ungrateful. Being ungrateful is a human description of certain behaviours and humans understand when they have been ungrateful and the likely consequences of this. Fred was probably just doing what he had learned worked for him and thus repeated his behaviour.*

ii. *Dogs that are generally the decision makers within an established natural domestic/feral dog group do not generally act in such an aggressive way all the time towards their group members.*

iii. *Fred was also bought up as a young puppy in a house with 12 other Westies and a whole heap of children so it was unlikely that he didn't get enough contact with humans at a young age.*

iv.   Not <u>all</u> Westies show this behaviour.

It was more likely that Fred had learned that if he growled and bit people he got what he wanted, to be left alone and not bothered with. He rarely encouraged interactions with his owners and seemed to prefer being left alone. When he barked at the birds and the aeroplanes they went away and thus Fred's aggressive behaviour was constantly being reinforced. Fred would have had no concept that the plane was going to fly over whether he barked or not anyway.

When Fred barked, so did his owners by yelling "SHUT UP FRED"! By shouting at him he may have believed they were also barking at this annoying threat. He may have also begun to associate bad things happening to him when these threats appeared. After all his owners seemed to be having a bad time, he was getting punished and it was jolly hard work having to shout a lot. This may have made him even more determined to get rid of them the next time around.

What we did

i.   First of all it was important that Fred was given a thorough medical check by his vet to see if there were any clinical reasons why he did not like being picked up or touched. It turned out that in Fred's case he did have a problem with one of his kneecaps, which kept slipping out of place. It was kept an eye on and pain killers given when necessary. A future operation was also discussed. Therefore, it was quite likely that Fred didn't like to be picked up for this reason and had learned some effective ways of making sure he wasn't. However, he wasn't always in pain and showed no aggressive problems with his groomer so there was probably more going on than first expected.

ii. *Since in "dog world" a show of strength is an important way of establishing yourself within your group it was feasible that Fred was having a few status issues regarding where he saw himself and where his owners would have liked him to be. Therefore, we made sure that we established some consistent basic ground rules and dealt with this issue by using a learn to earn game similar to the one described earlier in this book.*

iii. *The owners were advised not to tell him off when he showed any aggression and to ignore this behaviour.*

iv. *Since Fred liked his own space, he was given it but not at the expense of his owners. From now on Fred had his own escape area where he could go and relax, away from the family and well out of way of biting range. This was his very own area consisting of a covered dog bed and some chews.*

v. *During the learn to earn exercise, his owners began to teach him that being touched ended in reward. Therefore, as Fred was waiting for the instruction to "take it", his owners began to touch him very gently along his side away from the bad knee. If he reacted aggressively they got up and walked away and Fred received nothing. If he remained calm he got his reward a tiny piece of smoked sausage, Fred was very partial to a small piece of smoked sausage. Gradually over weeks the owners worked their way across his body and then began by using a small soft brush. Finally they got to the stage where they could pick him up but he was never very happy at them doing this. Dogs do not try pick each other up so why should we believe that all small dogs will enjoy this activity. Some do not, so leave them on the floor on four legs where they belong.*

vi. *The sofa was out of bounds and if he tried to jump up he was calmly led back down with the use of a house line.*

vii. *To help stop Fred doing himself a mischief every time a plane flew over, the owners were asked to call him inside using a jolly voice and to play the game with him. Soon Fred learned that the Boeing 747 departing from East Midlands airport at 15.35 to Malaga meant sausage time and soon began to look for his treat rather than giving the captain and his crew a helping hand.*

When the new baby arrived Fred learned that having it around was a good thing since his owners were too busy with it than bothering with him and that the odd sausage would magically appear. As the baby develops into toddler stage, however, it will be extremely importance that the two do not clash and that calming measures are put in place to keep them apart without either of them realising it. The situation is being managed with care; Fred has not bitten anyone up to date and is less reactive but is he cured of ever biting again? I don't think so.

Fred never became a cuddly dog and on occasion still acted like Victor Meldrew. He needed his space and sometimes his painkillers. He needed to have less stress around him and to understand exactly what it is he could and could not do. The confrontation he used to have with his owners has greatly reduced since they do not react back and Fred is not placed into that challenging situation any more. For Fred it's as good as it gets.

Scruffing?

It is not a good idea to grab a dog by the scruff and force it down. The area at the back of the neck is where another dog may try to grab and hold on to during a challenge and a hand grabbing at this area is dangerously close to the sharp end.

However, attempting to touch the back of a dog's neck is a very common behaviour shown by humans. Many people lunge toward a dog, smiling (showing teeth), making a funny noise and then grab the back of the dogs neck in attempt to stroke it. To some dogs this is highly challenging and even frightening. It's no surprise that some dogs bite. Of course then the person responsible will then cry "But I was only being friendly" but this is probably not what the dog is thinking.

It is much kinder to the dog not to challenge it at all. That also means not staring at it either. Simply ignore it and if you are a family friend, vet or a relative implement the learn to earn game after the dog has settled and has realised that you are not threatening.

The worse case scenario

Sometimes, however, there is not such a satisfactory ending and some dogs are beyond help and the inevitable happens. This happened to me whilst I was working at a local rescue centre. I was asked to see a man who had recently re-homed a Rottweiler called Maisey. I must admit when I first saw him I thought he had been involved in a road accident. His arms and neck were covered in bruises and he had a cut to his cheek.

Maisey's story:

Maisey had been taken away from her previous home by RSPCA officers. She had been shackled up outside in a back yard and her neck was rubbed raw from the chain. Maisey was pitifully thin and suffering from mange and flea infestation. It took many months before she was in any state to be re-homed. Thankfully her owners were successfully prosecuted.

During her recovery in the kennels she had been a model patient and had showed no signs of what was about to happen once she was re-homed. Her new owner fell in love with her and after passing a successful home check took her back to his home to begin a new life.

However, after a few days Maisey began to act oddly whist out walking when off the lead. "It was as if a red mist descended upon her and then her eyes would turn black" her new owner explained. She then proceeded to chase her new owner across the park nipping at his ankles. Of course a nip in Rottweiler terms can be quite nasty and he had to have three stitches the second time she did this. A few days later she ran towards him, grabbed at his arm and literally pulled him bodily across a playing field. Luckily there was someone also walking a large dog and between them they shouted and barked loud enough to distract Maisey.

Once home, Maisey became the nice dog her new owner had fell in love with. In fact within the home environment Maisey was a perfectly normal well mannered dog and showed no signs that anything was wrong. The owner decided he would try again but this time kept her on a long lead and for a few days all was fine. Since her behaviour had improved her new owner decided he would give it one more go and let her off the lead. She took off at great speed for some distance and then turned, the red mist descended and she flew towards her owner knocking him to the ground. She went for his shoulder, *tore a chunk out of it and again dragged him along the ground. After some time she let go and stood still allowing the owner to get up from the ground and put her back on her lead. He spent a few days in hospital and a week later reluctantly brought her back to the centre. Since I had not seen this behaviour for myself and had no wish to, I had to take the explanation of what happened as the truth. His explanation of Maisey's behaviour, the extent of his injuries and the tears in his eyes told me he was telling the truth and since Maisey could not be re-homed safely it was decided by rescue centre vet that she be put to sleep.*

This was a very rare case and veterinary checks may have come up with a more sinister explanation of why Maisey behaved in this way but under these circumstances it would have been unwise and dangerous to continue. I have only had to deal with a few exceptional cases in my career and thankfully this type of aggression is rarely seen.

If you are experiencing any sort of aggressive problems with your dog please ask the advice of a qualified and recommended companion animal behaviourist in your area. Most aggressive problem behaviour can be managed but beware of any "expert" claiming a "cure".

Chapter Nine

Loud noises and other such scary stuff.

Many owners dread the looming of November the 5th which nowadays seems to begin in September and continues well on into the New Year. The shelves during this time at the veterinary surgery become devoid of tranquilisers and the drug and pet companies benefit greatly by selling quick fix products. Meanwhile a host of shivering wrecks shake and tremble behind sofa's. Then during the spring and summer the warm weather brings us thunder storms, builders, bird scarer's and guns. Life can become very stressful living with a nervous dog all year round.

So why are some dogs such scardy cats?

Well once again there are lots of reasons why some dogs can't cope with loud noises and other such scary stuff.

- It may be due to their genetic make up, they are simply nervous dogs.
- Some particular breeds of dog can be more nervous than others.
- The dog may not have been exposed to loud noises as a young puppy.
- The dog may have learned to associate a particular noise with a bad experience.
- There may be a clinical reason, so it is important that if the behaviour suddenly occurs for no obvious reason a full medical check up is carried out.

It is important that each dog is assessed individually to try and find out the underlying causes of its nervous behaviour so we can correctly diagnose and design the appropriate behavioural modification programme.

How can I tell if my dog is really nervous of loud noises?

Body language and posture is a great indicator of how nervous your dog may be feeling. A slightly nervous dog will show a lowered body carriage, its tail may be pointing down and its ears may flatten against the head. It will actually look like it is nervous. A more fearful dog may crouch lower, its tail may curl under the body and the ears may become a lot more flattened to the head. A really fearful dog may crouch quite flat and quiver on the floor. Its tail will be firmly clamped beneath its body and its head will be turned away with the ears firmly flattened against it. It may make a whimpering sound, shake, roll over or even urinate and will probably try to scurry away and hide. It will show these types of postures whilst the stimulus is occurring. However, the dog may also learn that certain situations trigger these scary situations. For instance a drop in air pressure may indicate to a dog that thunder is inevitable as the two go together and will begin to act nervously before the sound occurs. Some even associate the onset of dark evenings with the arrival of fireworks. Just because you can't see a reason for why your dog may be suddenly acting nervously, your dog may have a very good one indeed.

What can we do to help a dog cope better with loud noises?

We can teach our dog that the noise is actually not so scary after all by desensitising it and using counter-conditioning techniques.

Densensitising and counter-conditioning

Owners that seek professional help will often be advised to desensitise and counter-condition. So what does this actually mean?

Desensitisation is when the stimulus that causes the problem behaviour is brought closer and closer in small steps to the dog over a very long period of time. If the stimulus is noise this can start at a very low volume and gradually the volume increased. However, you only move on to the next step once the dog remains calm at that level of stimulus.

To help speed up the process of desensitisation, counter-conditioning can be used which helps the dog to associate the problem forming stimulus (initially at a low intensity) with performing a more pleasant behaviour which is incompatible. For instance, the dog may be offered a treat and it would perform eating behaviours rather than nervous ones.

To help explain these techniques more clearly I will describe the case history of Ben an adorable Springer Spaniel puppy.

Bens Story:

I first met Ben a few years ago whilst working in South Yorkshire. His vet had referred him as Ben was very frightened of loud noises and in particular bangs. He had showed this behaviour ever since his owners acquired him from the breeder. This particular breeder specialised in training and breeding gun dogs and his way of testing puppies to see if they were gun shy (afraid of a gun firing) was to place them in a field and have several gun shots fired. If they reacted in a nervous way he would sell them as pets and if they didn't he would train them up as gun dogs. Ben reacted badly so was sold at the ripe old age of 18 weeks to his present owners. He had come to his new owners straight from a rather barren kennel and into a home environment and soon began to shake, shiver and urinate every time the vacuum cleaner appeared, or the door slammed or the children came racing down the stairs. The owners put this down to Ben not being properly socialised to indoor conditions and tried to show him all was well by using reassuring words and cuddles every time he showed this behaviour.

Ben's owners, to their credit, had discussed and researched thoroughly which breed of dog they wanted as a family pet and, since they lived in the countryside surrounded by fields, thought that they could accommodate a lively working Springer Spaniel. However, later that year, when the pheasant season started the field suddenly became full of barber jackets, tweed hats and of course loud bangs. Ben just couldn't cope and spent all day quivering in a puddle of urine behind the sofa.

So to help Ben cope better we put in place some desensitising and counter conditioning techniques. But before we could do this we had to wait for the guns to go away. Once all was quiet for that season we used a specific CD which was designed to produce bang noises (see back of this book for website details of where to find CD's of fireworks, thunder and traffic noise).

Initially the volume was kept so low that Ben did not react and whilst the CD was playing Ben was given nice things to do, such as playing with a toy or sitting for a treat. Then over weeks and months the volume was gradually increased in very small steps but only when Ben was relaxed with the stage he was at. He soon learned that the quiet banging noises meant that nice things happened to him and gradually he coped better and better as the bangs increased in intensity. The owners were also asked not to reassure Ben by cuddles and "there there" words when he was frightened, since these may be reinforcing his nervous behaviour. Therefore, they had to remain calm and show Ben they were not bothered by going about their daily routine.

This technique worked well and Ben does not react to low quality bangs such as doors slamming and children running about. However, at the height of the shooting season Ben is still a little wary and is taken elsewhere for his walks.

Ben would have never made a "perfect" gun dog even though he was supposedly bred for it. Believe it or not lots of so called gun dogs do not make the grade and are sold as pets. Just because you have a breed that has been designed to fulfil a certain role don't be too surprised if it too does not make the grade. To find a great working sheep dog, a fabulous gun dog or one that dances a waltz many puppies are bred, tested and fall at the first post.

De-sensitising and Counter-Conditioning may be used for helping nervous dogs to cope with other fearful situations such as thunder, fireworks, traffic noise and are also useful tools to help dogs cope with car journeys, visiting the vet and other dogs or people.

If you are experiencing problems with nervous behaviour ask the help of your local qualified behaviourist.

Chapter Ten

Dealing with poor recall problems.

Not all dogs come back when called and some will run away from you which can lead to problems regarding safety if you can't stop your dog from rushing towards a busy road.

So why can't some owners get their dog back?
- ➢ The dog may not understand that you actually want it to come back.
- ➢ Others ignore you since they have learned that nothing much happens to them if they do.
- ➢ They may become so excited by the appearance of a cat, person or another dog that nothing much else matters.
- ➢ And some simply don't want to come back because when they do their owners shout at them.

It does not necessarily mean?
- ➢ Your dog is running in front because it views itself as the "top dog" and is leading the pack and that you should make more of an effort to stay in control.
- ➢ That your dog is purposely winding you up to annoy the hell out of you.
- ➢ That you are a bad owner and your dog is trying to escape.

So how can we improve our dogs recall?

1. Just because we shout really loudly "**come back!**" It doesn't mean that our dog understands what this actually means. Coming back is quite a complicated concept to get your head around especially if your brain is not designed to cope with such cognitive skills. Therefore, you have to teach your dog what "come back" actually means. This entails constantly repeating the word "come" whilst the dog is actually coming towards you. If the dog is rewarded every time it comes back it will soon put two and two together and learn to associate "come" with moving towards you and will <u>want</u> to perform this behaviour because it gets rewarded for doing so. Behaving as if you were the top dog will not teach your dog what the word "come" actually means.

2. Some dogs understand very well what the instruction to "come" means but make an informed decision to ignore you because they have learned that nothing much happens to them if they do. Therefore it is a good idea to teach your dog that nice things happen to them if they do come back. So every time your dog returns, reward it with a tasty treat, a toy or a fuss. If your dog decides that treats, toys or a fuss are not worth coming back for, make sure you stop your dog learning that he can get away with that by using a long line plastic washing line or horse lunge line. Then if your dog ignores your instruction, firmly without any fuss reel your dog in. Having a dog on a long lead also means you can keep your dog safe from charging across busy roads and railway lines.

3. Make sure that you are more exciting than cats, rabbits, other dogs and people by having with you something your dog really loves. This could be a tasty treat, a ball or a Frisbee. Produce this reward at intermittent times throughout the walk to keep your dog interested in you.

4. Some owners reprimand their dogs for not coming back to them after they already have. Dogs can not possibly understand the concept of punishment after the event. They might look sheepish and guilty but this is because they know you are cross with them. What they won't necessarily understand is why. Therefore, what the owner is doing is punishing their dog for coming back. If your dog comes back after the event there is not much you can do but carry on with the walk preferably to the nearest pet-store to buy a long training line.

The teenage months

As with all training the earlier you start the better. However, there may come a time in your dog's life when it begins to act rather like a stroppy teenager. This usually happens as the dog is beginning to mature and it is during this time that many dogs end up in rescue centres. Your dog may suddenly seem to forget what the word "sit" means or "wait" and may begin to show selective hearing. This is when it cannot hear you say "come" but can hear a packet of crisps being opened half a mile a way. Do not be too disheartened, remain resolute and consistent and stock the fridge with a few bottles of Sauvignon Blanc. Hopefully in a few months time you may get your original dog back again. If not seek advice.

Quick fixes

Some dog trainers may encourage the use of a shock collar or another punishing device to quickly fix this problem. The dog is punished with a shock from its collar as it runs away. It may be running towards another dog for instance. So what does the dog learn? It learns that running towards other dogs is a bad thing to do since it gets hurt. For a few times after this the dog may stop running towards other dogs. However, it may also learn that other dogs appearing on the scene equals a shock so may begin to form a very negative association with them. This may cause the dog to start to show aggressive behaviour towards approaching dogs in an attempt to get rid of them. Or the dog may begin to show fearful behaviour in the presence of other dogs. But does your dog learn to come back? Just because you may have stopped your dog running away does not mean that you have taught him the true meaning of "come back". The real danger of this approach is when the inexperienced dog owner shocks the dog at the wrong time. This can caused fear and confusion and a very unhappy hound.

It's surely better to have your dog come back to you because it wants to not because it has to.

Chapter Eleven

Inappropriate elimination within the home.

Another common reason why dogs end up in rescue centres is inappropriate elimination within the home. The dog may have suddenly stated to urinate and/or defaecate in areas you do not want them to. There are many underlying factors for this and include:

- ❖ Medical problems.
- ❖ Age related problems.
- ❖ A lack of toilet training.
- ❖ A preference for a certain substrate.
- ❖ Anxiety problems for instance, when being left alone.
- ❖ The dog trying to increase its sense of security and topping up its own familiar scent.
- ❖ Over-marking for territorial or status reasons.

It may be one, partly or all of these reasons and the question of why it is eliminating inappropriately needs to be addressed before the behaviour is modified.

1. Firstly it is important that your dog has a full medical examination since many elimination problems are due to a number of clinical problems. Once your vet has ruled this out they can refer you on to a qualified behaviourist.

2. It may be that your dog is simply getting older and can't get where it should be going quickly enough. Your vet may also be able to help as there are lots of ways to help improve quality of life for the older dog but you can also make sure that your dog has easy access to appropriate areas. It is also important not to become cross or anxious with your dog for something that it can't control.

3. It may be that you have rescued a dog and it simply hasn't been shown where it can and can not go. Remain patient and keep popping your dog onto the substrate you wish it to go on. If it looks like your dog is going to perform indoors, firmly say "no" but remain calm and take your dog to where you do want it to go. The more often a dog eliminates on a particular substrate and associates this with the relief of an empty bladder the better the chance you have of successful toilet training.

4. It may be that your dog has only learned to go, for instance, on the carpet. Therefore, has learned a preference for that substrate by a classical conditioned response. Some dogs will only perform on that particular substrate and nowhere else. To help your dog change to a different substrate use an old piece of the preferred substrate, e.g. carpet and gradually move it nearer to the back door until it you can get the dog outside. Then gradually add very small increasing amounts of the preferred substrate such as soil over a period of weeks until the dog slowly becomes conditioned to the new substrate.

5. Some dogs when left alone become anxious and this may result in them wanting to urinate or defaecate. To help them cope better with being left see Chapter Five.

6. A dog may be feeling insecure and may feel the need to familiarise itself within the home. It may be that a new carpet has been laid or a new sofa has been delivered. In this case you can help familiarise these new objects by rubbing an old towel over the dog and then transferring the scent to the new furniture.

7. Other dogs may urinate in areas to top up their own scent. It may be in response to an unfamiliar dog or person within the house and some dogs even urinate up against shoes or shopping bags that may smell unfamiliar. This may mean that the dog has some status or anxiety issues within the home these will need to be addressed.

Classical conditioning

This is a learning process whereby the dog learns by association to pair two or more things together. For instance if a bell was rung and after a few seconds tasty food appeared the dog would soon begin to predict the arrival of food and begin to salivate in anticipation. Hence the reason why many dogs begin to get excited and salivate when the "neighbours" tune is played on the TV since many dogs are fed just after. This type of learning is involuntary since the dog can't make itself salivate. Learning a substrate preference to eliminate on is another.

Operant conditioning

This type of learning is where the dog learns a behaviour usually by trial and error and the dog gets rewarded for it so will repeat it the next time. Some dogs are great at opening doors. It looks like a clever trick but what the dog has done is jumped up and down trying to escape and has inadvertently knocked the handle, this worked thus the dog repeats it the next time. The dog has not sat looking at the door thinking "Ah yes to open this door, first I must reach up with my paw and yes I must then turn the handle and take a step back". It is simply that by performing a certain behaviour the dog gets a result.

Bobs story:

Bob was a lovely little Jack Russell Terrier cross who was obtained by his present owners from an elderly couple. The elderly couple became breeders by accident when they left a back door open whilst their own female Jack Russell was in season. An unknown intruder entered the premises and left with a smile, leaving no clues to his parentage. Consequently the little Jack Russell gave birth to nine puppies and they all lived happily in the front room (it was a very small bungalow with little outside space) until re-homed between the ages of eight and eighteen weeks of age. Unfortunately Bob was one of the last to go and had busily been performing his toileting duties all over the front room carpet. Try as they might his new owners could not stop him from doing this as he simply would not go to the toilet outside.

Bob had formed a preference for only going on carpet so we had to change his preference to some other substrate. Since the new owners had a large lawn it was agreed that would we try to change his preference from carpet to grass instead. A large piece of old carpet was rescued from the back of their garage, cut into sections and placed inside a large plastic tray used for stacking bread. This was placed in the front room and Bob happily used it. If he began to sniff around another part of the carpet he was gently placed onto it. Gradually the tray was pushed closer to the kitchen and then finally out of the back door. This was not a very hygienic approach but better than having to clear up the mess daily from the lounge carpet. Once the tray was outside, a small piece of lawn turf was placed onto it and over time more pieces were used so that eventually turf covered the whole tray. Once Bob was re-conditioned to using the tray plus turf the tray was removed and Bob continued to use grass from then on. This process took over six weeks *to achieve but the owners were very patient and very committed. They now have a nice dog and a nice carpet.*

What Bob was <u>not</u> doing was acting as if he was a "top" dog and marking his territory to gain some sort of dominance over his owners.

What about rubbing my dogs noses into it?

<u>Never rub a dogs' nose into anything</u>, since it may cause injury. All it will achieve is to make the dog associate toileting with something bad. The dog may then try and hide it or just not go when the owner is present. Showing dogs things does not work. If you could teach dogs by showing them how to do things most dogs would be making the tea and picking the kids up from school. Dogs do not learn this way.

If you are experiencing inappropriate elimination with your dog ask the advice of a recommended behaviourist and they may be able to help you find the reasons why and explain what you can do to alleviate the problem.

Chapter Twelve

Coping with dogs that fight in the home.

Some dogs simply do not get on and world war three breaks out as soon as they get together. It is especially distressing when two dogs brought up happily as puppies suddenly begin to fight. As usual there are many different reasons why this may occur:

❖ The dogs may have begun to mature and are competing over what they view as one or more important resource.

❖ One or both dogs may have been poorly socialised with other dogs.

❖ They might associate each other in a negative way since every time they get close the owner starts to behave anxiously or may get cross.

❖ One or both may have had negative experiences with other dogs living with them.

❖ There may be a medical problem.

It is important that a clear and extensive history is taken to understand fully why the dogs are behaving aggressively towards each other since different reasons may warrant different modification procedures.

1) One of the most common underlying reasons is that the dogs have started to mature and begin to fight over resources that they find important. The use of a video camera comes in useful as the dogs can be viewed whilst the owner is not present. This will allow a better assessment of what the dogs may be competing over. If the dogs' only fight whilst the owners are nearby, it may be that they are competing over the owners themselves. Therefore, it is important that any status issues are addressed regarding where the dogs see themselves within the doggy/human group and that the owners are aware of how their behaviour towards the dogs may be affecting behaviour.

Just what might a dog view as an important resource?

Dinner or any food that may come its way.

The bowl its dinner comes in.

The water bowl or a place where the dog drinks.

A valued toy it may be all the toys or just one particular one.

A valued blanket or item of owners clothing.

A valued area to sit in, settee or chair or just anywhere it chooses.

A dog basket.

The owner's bed.

A doggy treat.

Its collar and lead.

A bone or rawhide chew.

Another family dog.

And very importantly some dogs really value their owners ATTENTION!

2) One or both of the dogs may not have been adequately socialised when young. They may have little understanding of how they are supposed to interact with other group members in a sociably acceptable canine way. If this is the case it is difficult once the dog is over three –four months of age to re-create this critical learning period. Instead it is important that the owner helps teach the dog a more acceptable way of behaving and will probably require some professional guidance.

3) If an owner becomes tense and uncomfortable (for whatever reason) around their dogs when they are together, this may result in the dogs learning to associate each other in a negative way. Therefore, make sure you act how you wish the dogs to act, in a quiet and calm fashion.

4) If one of the dogs has previously had a negative experience of other dogs living with them, it is important to teach this dog that other dogs are actually nice things to have a round. A de-sensitising program can be put in place where the problem dog is gradually introduced to the other dog in very small but positive stages.

5) To make sure there are no clinical reasons why a dog suddenly begins to show aggression, a full medical check is advised. If the vet is happy that the dog is well they may refer it to a recommended qualified companion animal behaviourist.

To illustrate how complicated dog-dog aggression is I will describe two case studies where aggression between familiar dogs occurred but for two very different reasons.

Jess and Blade's story.

Jess and Blade were two beautiful Weimaraner dogs who had been living relatively happily together until the older male dog Blade met with an unfortunate accident which resulted in a broken leg. When Blade returned home, presumably smelling of anaesthetic and vet hospitals, Jess the female dog acted as if she did not recognise him and behaved aggressively towards him. Normally Blade would have put Jess in her place but due to his injury deferred to her and from then on Jess persistently challenged Blade at every opportunity she could. She often took hold of his damaged leg and would try to bowl him over. At first the owners tired to keep them apart but this was difficult with two such big dogs and in the end Blade went to recuperate at a friend's house.

Finally when all was healed Blade was introduced back into the house but Jess was having none of it. Blade still tried to defer to her but Jess would not stop at that and would still constantly grab at his bad leg.

It would seem that Blade had lost some confidence in his ability to win a fight because of his injury and instead of challenging Jess he backed down. Once Blade had deferred to Jess she should have left him alone but for some reason she would not. The owners obtained Blade as a puppy and they had spent a great deal of time taking him to puppy school and out and about. However, they had acquired Jess from a rescue centre and had been given no previous history except that her owners were moving house, so why she was behaving like this was unclear. It may have been simply part of her nature, a lack of early socialisation or because it was making her feel good. Winning gives us a good feeling and there is no reason that dogs can't feel this way either.

To help re-establish the status quo the two dogs were brought back together gradually. Initially outside the home environment and eventually back inside. Blades scent was introduced back into the house by wiping an old towel that he had been sleeping on around the house. The towel was also placed beneath Jess's food bowl to help her associate his scent with nice things happening to her. The owners also made sure they were not seen as resources by introducing a learn to earn programme and Blade finally became more confident once he regained his strength from the operation. If Jess became too boisterous she was calmly moved away from him using a house line. Both dogs were reintroduced successfully and things are almost back to normal. Blade regained much of his old confidence but Jess still challenges him on occasion just in case.

Mavis and Floss's story.

Mavis was a five year old rescued Rottweiler who had been kept in a shed for the first three years of her life where she had apparently given birth to four or five litters of puppies. She was very thin and had to be treated for a heavy flea and mite infestation. She had been neutered by the rescue centre before she was put up for re-homing.

Floss was a four year old neutered terrier cross that the owners had also rescued before they acquired Mavis. Floss had been previously living with an elderly couple that had to give her away as they were moving to sheltered accommodation. For the first few months Floss and Mavis seemed to get along very nicely. However, one day the owners returned home to find blood all over the front room walls and Floss greeted them with half her ear missing which had to be stitched. A few weeks later the owners heard an almighty squealing from the kitchen where the two dogs were having their dinner. Once again Floss's ear was bleeding and had to be stitched up for a second time.

A few days later whilst the owners were handing out dog biscuits Mavis suddenly turned on Floss and went to bite her ear again. Floss, however, growled back at Mavis and ran away with her biscuit grumbling furiously. Mavis went towards Floss and snatched the biscuit away from her. A fight ensued and the owners had a hard job to separate them.

Mavis's behaviour worsened over the next few weeks especially around feeding times and the two dogs were kept apart during this period. The two dogs were clearly competing over food and even though Mavis was clearly the bigger and stronger dog Floss had decided that she wanted to keep her share.

The two dogs did not compete over any other issue just food. This desire for food may be understandable in Mavis's case since she had probably spent most of her life feeling very hungry and had learned to take what she could when she could. Since Mavis was also a big dog she had probably learned that she could use her physical strength to take it away from Floss. Floss on the other hand showed more tenacity, a typical terrier breed characteristic, and had decided not to give up her food without a fight. However, since Mavis was such a strong dog Floss was coming off worse and things were starting to get serious.

The owners were distraught and stopped all treat giving and made sure no food was available. The dogs were fed in separate areas and this worked for a few weeks. However, the dogs began to anticipate food times and began to become aggressive with each other before dinner time. They had also began to fight if one found a tiny crumb of something on the floor and food became even more of an issue. They gave up and sought help.

To help make food less of an issue we made it more available and a bit boring. The dogs were given their food little and often at random times through out the day but only after they had sat and waited until told to take it. The dogs were given complete dried food only and the dried food pieces were used as treats. The dogs were not able to anticipate when the food was coming as the owners made sure their behaviour was not triggering a response and the food just kept coming and coming.

Since the dogs were similar in strengths with neither backing down no one dog was treated first over the other. Instead the owners made sure that they were viewed as the stronger members of the group and they achieved this by using non-confrontational methods such as initiating interaction, ignoring attention seeking behaviour and by implementing a learn to earn programme.

The owners <u>manage</u> the situation and the two dogs have not had a fight since and can be left together as long as there is no food around. But it is important to realise that they are not "cured" of it <u>ever</u> happening again and the owners have to be forever vigilant.

Bitch Aggression

Fighting over resources amongst female dogs of similar strengths can often be amongst the most extreme aggressive behaviour that can occur. It is probably why we so often use the word "bitch" in a derogatory sense. In some extreme cases they are simply never to get along so unless you are prepared to split your house in two it would be a wise move to re-home one of them. After all why force them to live together if they really do not want to.

Chapter Thirteen

Other common problems; why does my dog sniff at other peoples crotches, pinch my pants, and roll around in sheep pooh?

Crotch sniffing

Billy Connolly once famously remarked that no book on dog behaviour ever taught him how he could stop his dog from sniffing other people crotches. My reply to this Billy is next time buy a dog with shorter legs.

Dogs live in a scented world. Just as we are surrounded by words that communicate things to us, the smells surrounding dogs are stuffed with important doggy information. Dogs naturally sniff around each others bottom area since this is where scent is more concentrated and thus, if they can reach, tend to sniff humans there as well. It may be embarrassing to a human since we tend to greet unfamiliar others at the other end of an outstretched arm, as far from the smelly area as possible. For a dog however, it gets all the information it needs right there in one big sniff to the crotch. If you have to stop your dog from pressing its nose against Auntie Flo's plaid skirt use a more interesting item to distract the dog. If you make it an issue and punish your dog every time Auntie Flo arrives for tea, your dog may do more than just sniff at her next time around.

Pant pinching

You may wonder why your dog spends a great deal of time and effort waiting for a chance to grab hold of your pants and run off with them. They are usually not your best pants and it can get quite embarrassing when they are taken out into the garden and displayed in full view of the neighbours. It doesn't have to be pants; it may be socks, bras, tee-shirts or shoes. It is usually something that you wear intimately and that happens to be a handy size that fits readily into the mouth. Vets all over the world spend a great deal of their time retrieving bits of cloth from the inner reaches of a dog's intestine.

So why do they pinch items of smelly clothing? As usual it could be for a number of reasons. It may be that they get comfort from being close to the strong scent of their owners. For others they may like the taste. For some it may be a great way of getting their owners attention and to make them chase them around the garden. It may seem to your dog that since you have taken great pains to rub your scent all over this item it must be of great importance to you, so they want it.

Therefore, in the future do not leave your dirty laundry lying around on the floor and don't chase your dog around the garden when it has a pair of your big salmon coloured knickers hanging from the corner of its mouth. Instead turn your back and busy yourself with a bag of nice doggy treats. Since these are now of number one importance your dog will probably drop your knickers and want the treats instead. Inconspicuously pick up the soggy item of clothing and put it out of reach. You can then give your dog something more appropriate to do after it has sat and waited for it.

Rolling and eating sheep pooh.

To most owners watching their dog consume vast quantities of sheep pooh and then rolling in it simply turns their stomachs. Of course it doesn't have to belong to a sheep, it may be deer, horse or even a cow pat. Dogs seem to gravitate towards pooh and devour it like it's been prepared by Gordon Ramsey and wear it like a Channel suit. It isn't very nice for us but for some reason dogs like it. There are many theories to why;

- ❖ It helps their digestive system
- ❖ It increases their scent
- ❖ It disguises their scent
- ❖ It helps the dog hunt since it carries the scent of the prey with it.
- ❖ It helps them to be sick.

If you do not want your dog to roll in sheep pooh then keep away from fields containing sheep. If you live on a sheep farm try and distract your dog with something more interesting instead. Or just let them get on with it in small doses and be prepared with gloves and a hose.

Conclusion!

Contrary to the old adage it's not always the owners fault. There are many underlying factors to why dogs behave the way they do. Sometimes it is a real problem bought about by lack of enriched early environment, flawed training regimes, learned behaviour or genetic variations. At others times the dog may be behaving normally but we as humans do not find this sociably acceptable. And yes sometimes the owner does not help matters by unintentionally reacting in the wrong way due to lack of communication or mis-understanding.

Trying to achieve perfection from our dogs depends very much on how we perceive perfection in the first place. We do not have to be seen to have the perfect dog in the eye of others. If our dog is happy and we are happy with our dog then so be it.

I hope this book has helped to make clear how complicated some problems can be and how important it is to come to a correct diagnosis when dealing with them. Simply stating that the problem must stem from the fact that the dog is behaving in as "Top dog" in a dominant fashion is not constructive advice for most problems that may occur. Trying to force a dog to behave like a human is now viewed as somewhat barbaric in today's world. Instead we are starting to look at how dogs behave naturally with each other and to use this ever increasing knowledge to help us and our dogs cope better and live happily ever after.

Useful Addresses

The Association of Pet Behaviour Counsellors (APBC)

PO Box 46

Worcester

WR8 9Y5

www.apbc.org.uk

The Companion Animal Behaviour Therapy Study group (CABTSG)

www.cabtsg.org.uk

Association for the Study of Animal Behaviour (ASAB)

www.asab.nottingham.ac.uk

Sounds Scary

11 Cotebrook Drive

Upton

Chester

CH2 1RA

www.soundscary.com

www.puppyschool.co.uk

Published by Rosie Barclay 1st Edition

Printed by www.lulu.com

Copyright: © 2007 Standard Copyright License

ISBN   978-0-9555881-0-5